Surviving in Between
Lorenzo Easterly Williams

Copyright © 2017 Lorenzo Easterly Williams

All rights reserved. No part of this book may be reproduced or transmitted in any form or by any means, electronic or mechanical, including photocopying, recording or by any information storage and retrieval system, without permission in writing from the publisher.
GoldenClock Publishing – Houston, TX
ISBN: 978-0-9995331-0-9
Library of Congress Card Control Number: 2017917147
Surviving in Between | Lorenzo E.Williams
Available Formats: eBook | Paperback distribution

About the Author

Lorenzo Easterly Williams was born in Knoxville Tennessee. He was raised in a community named Walter P Taylor Homes. He graduated High School in 1998 from Austin East High School. He later went on to college at the University of Tennessee at Chattanooga where he has a Bachelors degree in Finance. Lorenzo moved to Houston Texas 2 years after graduating High School and that is where he currently resides. He obtained a Masters Degree from Prairie View AM University in 2006 in Education Administration. Lorenzo Williams has been a school teacher in the Houston Texas area. Lorenzo has had to overcome many life's challenges. Through all of his life's challenges his faith has remained strong. He authored the Book Surviving in Between to be an inspiration and hope to many people facing various challenges.

Introduction

Sometimes, life will throw you a curve ball. Different things can happen; you can wake up and find yourself in unfamiliar situations. Take my life for example, the last 4 to 5 years of my life I've wrestled with loneliness and feeling like I was not living up to my standards. Sometimes during those curve balls of life, you have to dig deep and find your fight. Whether you find yourself in prison, a bad marriage, financial problems or health problems, you must dig deep within yourself and know you are an overcomer. Many times we are disappointed in ourselves for the life we have created. There's one thing about disappointment, it can be turned around if you have faith.

There may be times in life that you will feel empty inside and may lose your will. Life will give you some traumatizing blows and you may think you won't be able to overcome it. During those rough times in your life, it is important to not lose your will to survive. Sometimes the pain in our life will come to humble us and help us develop a better faith in Jesus. One thing I've learned in life is it is important to forgive people who've hurt you, no matter how bad. It's important for you to forgive them for your own peace of mind. Many times in life problems and depression can hit you from every angle. One could be your faith being tested in certain situations. At times, we bring upon our own wrong deeds. These things can hit you out the blue and you don't understand why a certain situation happened. During times of confusion it is important to try to listen to our spirits to see what the good lord is telling us. Life is never as bad as you may perceive. There is always someone worst off than you out there.

One important thing in life is to never forget how blessed you are and how much Jesus cared for you.

Many people give up on life and surrender to depression or whatever their addiction or habit is, I want to tell you from experience never give up or surrender. You must survive in between, even if you're going through a health challenge, legal matter or mental problem. Whatever your situation is it's important to have the right frame of mind. I've been through a lot of difficult situations and the one thing that helped to me was prayer and listening to the word of God. I tune out rap music because when you are going through trials and tribulations it is good to be in-tune with Jesus. Many people suffer in silence without any outlet and that's not a good thing.

Chapter 1
Getting Through Situations

One thing that could help depression is helping other people. Doing volunteer work in the community will make you feel better because you made a difference.

Sometimes we smile like everything is fine, no one really knows the struggles we are facing. One of the Bible verses that I like is in Deuteronomy 31:6 it says, "Be strong and courageous. Do not be afraid or terrified because of them, for the lord your god goes with you."

No matter how bad it seems, we serve a God that has made us promises and he loves us. Life will have its fair share of ups and downs, we must remain encouraged at all times. You can use the pain you experience in life as a testimony to help someone else overcome life challenges. One of the reasons I wrote this book was to encourage people who are dealing with different sets of situations. The thing about about trials and tribulations are they come to test who you really are. Everything that happens to us in life will not be understood. Sometimes it's karma coming back on us for something we may have did in the past. Maybe we did nothing. Problems can happen to anyone one of us; whether you're living good and perfect, or if you're doing stuff you know you have no business doing.

If you pray and have faith you can overcome any situation.

The lord speaks to us through situations and if we sit still we can hear the lord speaking to our spirits. You can make it though any storm or situation if you have the right mentality and stay prayed up. Find something you enjoy doing and do it. Whether it's being around friends, listening to your favorite song, getting your hair and nails done-do it until you feel better about your situation. Never give up or surrender; always fight for your happiness and peace of mind.

Sometimes in life you can feel a void, like everything seems to be falling apart. More than likely feeling helpless about a particular situation. Another passage of scripture that I like comes from Mathew 7:7, "Ask and it shall be given. Seek and you shall find, knock and the door shall be open."

It's easy! The good Lord specifically tells us to ask him. Ask him for wisdom and guidance in every situation you encounter. If you are worrying day in and day out and feeling hopeless, it is important to pray and get involved in a church to be around good people. There have been times in my life that I've been on trial and didn't understand where it came from. I've tried to figure it out, I don't understand. I realized God takes us through different trials to grow our strength in him. In Proverbs 3:5, the Bible says, "Lean not to your own understanding. Everything we will not understand."

Sometimes in life you will feel alone and isolated. The burdens of life are enough to weigh anyone down. Which is why it's important to spend time in prayer and listening to the word of God. "The word is a lamb unto my feet," Psalms 119:105.

In life you go through things so deep that you don't want to be around anyone and you yourself don't know what's wrong, you do know something is wrong. It doesn't matter if you have money, or not, prayer and spending time with the Lord works every time. Even when we are unsure of the direction to take or the decision to make, it is important to listen to that silent spirit and let the good Lord speak to you. We are living in challenging times, so it's imperative to have your mind focused. You can do this by listening to the Word, working out and doing whatever things you enjoy.

Some situations in life will hit us out the blue. We may be facing the loss of a job, false criminal charges, death of a loved one or health problems. All of which are the perfect recipe for a storm. In these cases, nothing else works prayer. Prayer will protect you against the wishes of your enemies. It is wise to believe in the power of prayer. If you been praying and it seems like your prayers have not been answered, just hold on a bit longer. When we are going through the trails of life, we can sometimes feel abandoned by God. When you have been in tough situations in the past and prayer has delivered you, then you know prayer is real. So, don't pay attention to the God haters in the world.

I wrote this book as a living testimony of what prayer can do. People all over the world deal with different situations and problems each and every day. Life sometimes will put you in some uncharted water; many different things and situations could cause life turmoil. I don't know what the future will hold, I wrote this book to help you develop the right mindset to deal with whatever situation you are in between. A good attitude and a positive mindset will help you survive the many situations in life, along with prayer. Many things can arise whether you're going through a divorce, having money problems, legal situations or health problems. The important thing you must see is the opportunities that can change the present and then you must come back even stronger from it.

Each person reading this book is unique and face different problems in life; different people need different support systems. If you are somewhere reading this book and currently do not have a job, I would like to encourage you to do some volunteer work in and around your community. Doing volunteer work will keep you involved and active while you're wait for a job opportunity and you could learn skills and how to do different things along the way.

Chapter 2
The Blame Game

Never blame someone else for your failures in life. Take responsibility for your own mistakes and work on correcting them to become a better person.

Life requires us to stretch mentally, emotionally and spiritually. As the season and the weather changes, so does life and we must be in a position to deal with it. The right frame of mind is vital and needed in order to deal with change, so we can lower any disappointment and increase the opportunities. At times, struggles in life come and we assume we are doing something wrong. You simply cannot be doing everything right and living morally and still struggle with a certain situation in life. It's never good to focus on your failures; try to think of new and improved ways to do things going forward. There is an old saying, "There is more ways to skin a cat."

One thing you have to remember is that every person you come into contact with is fighting a battle you know nothing about. You are not the only one dealing with pain, there are people dealing with way more than you. We face complex challenges in today's world, that's why prayer is important for guidance and direction. Thinking positive and doing positive things for others helps us emotionally, knowing that we are making a difference. We must all deal with our problems in a constructive manner. It is important never to give into fear because it can make us paralyzed in life, fear can have us doing stupid things and not thinking properly. As African American people, we have been through a lot and our coping strategies are very strong. The last 10 Years or so we have seen the suicide rate increase amongst African Americans for many different reasons. Bad situations or circumstances can happen to anyone and it can lead to an emotional roller coaster. No matter how bad things may seem there is always light at the end of the tunnel. Never give up, always keep your head up and stay strong and encouraged.

When I think of the many struggles people face, I can relate. For instance, I had an insurance business that failed due to my mistakes. I have dealt with the ups and downs of life as an entrepreneur. I was a teacher for 6 years and had to go through my contract not being renewed. I have even dealt with legal problems being falsely accused of things. I could go on and on, my point is we must learn to survive in the midst of challenging situations. Some days we may not know how we're going to make it, with faith we can survive the hard times of life. Throughout history African Americans have been able to adapt in the face of major trauma and significant hardships. Sometimes it hits us in our lives to get closer to Jesus.

It is important to always to keep a clear mind when things are not going well. Many times we panic and draw our own conclusions when something happens. We shouldn't blame ourselves when situations happen that we don't like. For example, you get arrested for a crime you know you didn't do. Your mind might start turning on you saying, "I'm about to go to prison." Are you willing to blame yourself and accept all of this is your fault? You are innocent until proven guilty and all the facts must come out. The facts are that you have only been arrested. You must think with a clear mind on the situation.

There have been sometimes when I was in some tough situations and I panicked. These instances will have you start thinking all kind of things; a million things running through your mind each minute. One thing I've learned about tough situations is to trust the good lord with whatever you find yourself in. In life, we must learn from our mistakes and become wiser. We must also learn from other people's mistakes they've made and learned from.

To my brothers in prison or currently selling drugs, you must make a change. It is better to be free and broke, than to sell drugs and lose your freedom. The Lord has taken many people through different things for a reason. In the Bible Joseph was in prison, he was obedient to God while he was in prison. You can start off by going to church while you are in prison. Then, start staying away from gangs and the drama while you are in prison. The good Lord works in mysterious ways and he can open doors for you. We must learn to pass through difficult points in our life with a cheerful attitude. I know it's not easy to when you are locked in prison, but you must try.

There are many things you can go through: failing health, bad marriage, family problems, etc.. There are lessons to learn as we go through it all. The Lord tells us in the Word, Hebrews 13:5, "I will never leave thee, nor forsake thee." We've got to believe in his word and the power of his might. A major setback could be missing an opportunity to focus and propel you to greater heights.

Look at things on the brighter side and realize how you can change while going through the situation. I wrote this book by going through some bad circumstances. I had always wanted to, it wasn't until I went through some bad situations that I could. I took those bad situations I went through and started writing, it probably never would have happened if I didn't go through the fire. I decided to turn a bad situation around with a good attitude. Many times the Lord will talk with us through the many situations we face. We as people are resourceful and wise, so we must sit still and learn to keep our spirit on one direction to take when facing conflict. Never keep thinking of the bad and the things that could go wrong. Get into the Word of God, listen to the good preaching and teaching, volunteer to help a cause and keep your mind away from negative things.

If you are worrying about a particular situation, go do something productive-Go workout, get involved with church activities, hang out with your friends, go get a mani-pedi and focus your mind on good thoughts. The thing about listening to the Word of God is that when you are overwhelmed by a particular situation, the Word calms your worries. I know some people don't believe, I was tell them this, "If you die and you're not a believer, you have your soul to lose." It is wise to believe and have faith. Sometimes you will wake up in the middle of the night worried and wondering how you're going to make it through something seemingly impossible. You will play the worst-case scenario in your head. For instance, I am going to court in the morning for a crime I did not commit and they are going to lock me up.

Worrying is shows you do not trust Jesus to help you through your situation. Whatever challenging circumstances you find yourself in while you are reading this book, have faith. When my insurance company was having financial trouble, I spent many nights wondering how I was going to make it. Then, I did some stuff that got me in legal trouble. This was my fault; at the time I lacked good integrity and morals. I was disappointed in myself because I knew better. We must learn to forgive ourselves for the mistakes we've made. No one perfect and we all have some issues we must overcome. Prayer and meditation helps deal with the stress and fear of the unknown.

Moreover, procrastinating on things that need to get done is not beneficial to you. If you want to get out of the bad situation you are currently in, you must take action. If you are overweight or having health issues, you must take exercising seriously by going to the gym. If your business is not bringing in the money it once was, you must figure out where you can cut expenses. There are a lot of situations like these; you must always take positive action to correct them.

Chapter 3
Forgive and Move on

In life, not matter the setback you have encountered, you must always pick up the pieces and move on. No one in life is going to feel sorry for you. Out of all the evil and hurtful things that have happened to you in the past, you must get over. People generally do not like to be around someone that is complaining about life all the time. Have a humble spirit and be joyful because there are many people who have been through what you been though, and more.

The key is to forgive and you also must forgive yourself. It is important to not get stuck in the "why me" or the victim mentality. All of us will face different situations in life. We must view all situations as an opportunity to grow and become better.

If you don't have a job right now because of a criminal conviction, you could still volunteer your time to a cause. Sometimes volunteering can lead to a job or different opportunities. Look for actions you could take to become a better you. It's not good to focus on the negative of a situation, rather focus on where you can improve. One thing I have done to help myself is limiting how much news I watch. The news can be very depressing. So I focus on other things, like working out, volunteering or simply giving encouraging words to someone who may need it.

Difficult times or circumstances can happen to anyone; everyone goes through their own share of problems, so never feel like the lonely ranger. During these times, you must think of action plans that will help you get out of the mess you find yourself involved in. If you are in a bad marriage, you should think of the steps you could take to make the marriage better. For women, it could be any number of things, such as talking to your husband in a respectable tone, cooking for him or dressing sexy for him. Don't nag or start unnecessary fights. For further help, go to counseling or discuss how you all will deal with money and who takes care of what responsibilities. For men, it could be any number of things as well; honoring your commitment to marriage by not cheating, or if you go out then come in at a respectable time, work and bring something to the table. There are many examples of what makes a marriage work, going to church together also will help. This is just one example of a circumstance that could happen. On the surface, certain situations can look like a disaster and actually could be disastrous if all the focus is on the negative aspects. When we trust the Lord with all our heart, then our own understanding (although it may look rough in the beginning) will be that some good can come from what looked like a bad circumstance.

Be encouraged. We must own our mistakes and take actions to correct them. Don't waste your time blaming other people for your misfortunes. Also, you shouldn't sweat the small stuff in your life. Move on, forgive and become a better person. The only time we should look back at a situation is to reflect on how we could have handled the situation better; hindsight is always 20/20. When we're in certain situations we don't know how they will turn out, we must have faith in Jesus that it will work out fine. Stop beating yourself up for mistakes you've made in the past. Pray and forgive yourself and move on with your life.

Look, we are all human and we are perfectly imperfect. I have some homeboys that I grew up with in Walter P. Taylor homes in Knoxville, TN. They recently served a lot of time in prison for selling drugs. Sad to say, when they were release, they sold drugs again. What they don't realize is a critical mistake they're making. Not being caught again in whatever way, they are not learning from their mistake.

On the other hand, I also have friends that get out of prison, get jobs and realize what they were doing was wrong. They are now with and happily taking care of their families.

Chapter 4
Trust In Him, He Has Your Back

Be grateful for the things in your life. Let's start thinking of all the things to be thankful for: First of all, we woke up this morning; we have health, strength, family and friends that love us. Most of us have a car and a place to lay our heads. Be thankful for the little things in life as well. When times are bad, think of something you are grateful for.

In life all of us will face difficult times. We have those times where we are up all night worrying. In the Bible, 1 Peter 5:7, it says, "Cast your cares upon the Lord; for he careth for you. We must have faith and believe that whatever we are going through we will get through it. Some of us have overcome great odds and situations in life, i.e., having parents with drug and alcohol addictions, no parents, abused and a very many other things. Some of us have had anger toward family and/or family circumstances. Forgiveness, mediation and prayer can go a long way. We must pray, also work and attempt to forgive things so God can bless what we are trying to do.

It is foolish for someone to pray all day for a job, never goes to look for one. When we pray for that job we have to go knocking and looking for an opportunity. Keep the faith that you can overcome whatever obstacle you are currently facing and believe in the power of prayer and in miracles. No matter the situation, there is some good that will come from it. No matter where you are in life, be creative and determined to get back on track, if you are not. If you don't have a job right now, keep looking! Go and do some volunteer work to help the community. Volunteering will make you feel better about helping out; it gives you a sense of purpose.

We all have challenges and circumstances that we are dealing with, if you have a determined heart you can overcome any challenge. Here's an exercise that could help: write down a list of action steps each day. You could use it to help you overcome your current situation. Put it in your spirit that whatever is going on will not break your spirit. Determine to be happy with your life. Enjoy the small success as well as the large. Don't ever give up trying to achieve your goals. Whether it is losing weight, looking for a job, being a good parent or thriving in your marriage, never give up because the happiness will hit you.

Many times we think about things that have happened in our lives. We wonder if we would have done this or that, then this situation would have never happened. Whether you lost money, your home, marriage or whatever the situation may be we replay things in our mind. What happened in the past is the past; there is nothing that can be done about it. However, you can learn from the past to improve your tomorrow.

We all go through some tough situations in life. Sometimes you will feel down and hurt, you should stop feeling sorry for yourself and think of ways to improve. Use your life challenges and situations you have been in and use them as lessons learned for the future. No matter what has happened in the past don't let bitterness and un-forgiveness stop your blessings. Decide to be a good person through it all. I been through a lot of tough situations in life and one thing I learned is that through the good, bad, ugly and sad, whether it was my fault, or not, good can come from any situation. Hurdles in our lives will come, have faith we can overcome them always. Come up with action plans for defeating them when they do.

It is good to mediate, pray and focus on positive things and block out the negative. Booker T. Washington has a saying, "Success is to be measured not so much by the position that one has reached in life as by the obstacles which he has overcome." I'm sure many people reading this book has been laid off numerous times, went through a divorce or had to deal with family members on drugs. Some of us are facing challenges and get stuck in fear. Think of some of the things you had to do in order to overcome already. For example, you have a criminal record so it's tough to find a job. You either had to be proactive in your job searches or start a business, both requiring you to have confidence and patience in your ability. Others have went through a divorce and survived mentally and emotionally because of inner strength. Some of us had to be strong for family members and show them tough love and to help them understand that life is about growing and learning.

So, in your current situation, you can get strength from the past on how you overcame those challenges. We must learn coping skills to deal with rough times in life. Many times the challenges we go through in life helps us develop a closer relationship with God. Take the time to reflect on different situations you go through in your life and determine that you will not be a victim, a victor. Life has dealt you blows in the past and you survived. You will survive whatever challenge you face if you keep the faith in Him. Sometimes we have to calm our emotions down and thank God for the problems we don't have. If you give in to self-pity, anger and low self-esteem, you will give in to depression. If you give in to depression, you can give in to suicide. Fight!

There is always more than one way to handle a situation. Think of your options, write them down and pray on the best course of action for your situation. Make sure you are in the right spirit, mentally and emotionally. Taking care of yourself is important to deal with certain situations in your life. Working out will help with your stress levels; it also helps in your general health. If you are currently not working out, I encourage you to begin-Even if it is just walking around the neighborhood every morning. Examine where you spend your time, efforts and money. Look at what you are doing; this could be what is truly making you happy or sad.

We all from time to time make bad decisions in our lives. Sometimes we are simply in the wrong place at the wrong time. We must forgive ourselves as well as the people that hurt us. Don't let bitterness and unforgiveness live in your heart. When you do, it doesn't hurt anyone yourself. You can make it back from any situation as long as you have faith. People will come into your life and maybe in a rough season. Our life has many chapters and in some of them we may feel lost, confused and don't know which direction to take. In the Bible, Proverbs 3:5, it says, "Trust in the LORD with all your heart and lean not on your own understanding. That's why it's important to pray and ask the Lord for guidance. We don't always understand why things happen the way they do. Don't dwell on the bad situations you were in yesterday. Instead, get creative and come up with an action plan to achieve the desired results you were looking for. Imagine good things happening to you.

No matter what situation you find yourself in currently, there is light at the end of the tunnel. If you are in prison, you can make it home to enjoy your family and get your life back on track. If you are having health issues, you can get back in the gym, start eating better and reclaim your health. These are just two examples, understand and remember, no situation is permanent. When we are facing hardship we must have hope that things will get better. Without hope people would just give up on life. Weather the storm and fight the good fight, there is light at the end of the tunnel. One thing about the Bible is that God said, "He would never leave us or forsake us." We must get that down in our soul and spirit, no matter what situation we are facing. Hope will encourage you when you don't want to go on anymore. Don't feel like the lone ranger, meaning don't feel like you're the only one facing problems of different sorts. There are people who survived what you are going through, and even more. Make it up in your mind that you will be a survivor. Stress can kill and/or cause you some health problems, that's why coping skills are important.

Going to church, listening to the Word of God, working out and doing stuff you enjoy doing takes your mind off the things that stresses you out. Yes, hoping for that job is good, it's not enough; you should be proactive in trying to land a job by filling out some applications and networking.

Chapter 5
Having a Plan

I had been thinking about writing a book for a long time. Always procrastinated when it came to just sitting down and writing. Once I sat down and actually started writing it, my thoughts came together. The goal of any task you are trying to complete is to come up with an action plan and get it moving. There will be times when you will find yourself flat broke. The thing to remember is that you've been broke before and it was not the end of the world. Weep if you need to, get over it. Instead of soaking in misery, think of ways you can make money. Develop a plan of action on how you will go about putting money in your pocket. There are a lot of ways to get money! Avoid doing anything illegal because fast illegal money is a bad trap to nowhere, prison or death.

Some of the things we do in our lives we regret, we must forgive ourselves if we have asked the Lord to forgive us. Stretch yourself to keep learning and become a better you. In tough times you have to do what you have to do. If you can't find a job you might have to be a day laborer, or work at McDonalds. You have to do what you have to do in order to survive. You must let your pride go out the window.

I have a Bachelors degree from the University of Tennessee at Chattanooga and a Masters degree from Prairie View A&M University. Believe it, or not, I have been unemployed and broke before. Having a degree doesn't assure you that you will be employed. You must pray and keep in touch with the good Lord. There are people with Master's degree's out in the world that are homeless. Life will teach you to be grateful. Never take things for granted whether it's your spouse, job or health, have a grateful spirit and remain humble. Tough times will test your faith and your resolve. They don't last forever, tough people do. Stop crying, roll up your sleeves and get to praying. Not only that, get to doing what you have to do. Determine in your spirit that you will be resilient no matter what life throws your way.

Many of us have survived some tough circumstances in our childhood. Be determined not to let it break you. It should help you become a better you. In life, we don't want people to know how bad we struggle from time to time. We don't want people to know our marriage is falling apart, we lost our job or our business failed; we want the image of everything is good in our lives. We can't worry about what other people think of us and live life to the best of our ability.

Everyone you come in contact with in life is fighting a battle you know nothing about. Happiness doesn't come from material things, by serving and helping others will bring natural happiness. Don't ever feel like you are the only person having problems. There are lots of people dealing with all kinds of situations. Take time to reflect on things that happen day-to-day in our lives and try to learn from your mistakes. "Whenever you face trials of many kinds, because you know that the testing of your faith produces perseverance," James 1: 2-3.

Create some action plan steps to improve your current situation. Whether it is to improve your marriage, finding a job or just being happier in life. Be resilient and never give up hope that things could get better. Always keep your sense of humor, don't let life make you bitter and unhappy. Find things to laugh about and surround yourself with people who make you feel good. Everyone faces difficult situations from time to time. Think about some of the times you've overcome some difficult challenges already. Celebrate where you are at in life and how you have overcame the odds. Focus on the positives in life and get into the Word of God. Strengthen your mind with positive thoughts. Stay away from certain folks, your mind will become weakened being around negative people. I love rap music, it's not good for your mind, body or soul. Especially when you're dealing with different situations or there is a lot on your mind. Listen to the Word of God, read my book, read other inspirational books, go work out and keep your mind as strong as possible. Don't give into fear when you are facing situations. Have faith. Sometimes our minds will go in all kinds of different directions, especially when we are facing challenges. Always pray and give your problems to Jesus. There's something about when we pray and meditate that helps us deal with the storms of life.

One of the things that make me feel better is when I volunteer and make a difference in my community. Encourage and speak life over yourself. Block out the negativity! Talk to yourself and when it does come in your mind, speak life over your situation. When you feel yourself overwhelmed with worry and anxiety, go work out, read a good book or go talk to friends and family. Get active and give the Lord your worries. Many people want more stuff – cars, clothes, vacation and so forth. Unfortunately, when regular people can't keep up with rich people, they get depressed. Money doesn't always bring happiness; a lot of rich people kill themselves. What's really important is helping your neighbor, encouraging people that have lost their way.

Being kind to people is doing something to impact the world. Avoid being around gossiping people and people that are always complaining. Negative people will be a drain on your spirit. Stimulate your mind and your heart and every day. When you are facing trials and have circumstances in life you have to be especially careful what you feed your spirit. Sometimes you have to cut off the news and go spend time with a loved one. Go volunteer at a local place that needs help, read a good book or feed your mind with hopeful and positive vibes.

You may be in the valley, it seems like problems are all around you. Do not give into depression, this is when you fight and dig in. Fight for your happiness and peace of mind. Do something every day that is positive and that will help you get your life on the right track. If you want to go to school to get a degree in nursing, you must be proactive before you start. Research the school, go by and talk to the people there, apply for financial aid and research becoming a nurse. Little by little you will see yourself becoming a nurse. You can apply this to any situation. There is an old saying that the only thing that comes to a sleeper is a dream. So get out and get moving towards the direction you would like your life to go. One thing to remember is to pray for your direction and guidance. When deciding if you should move to a different city, date a person, or something about a job situation or business, always pray on it and listen to your spirit.

Have you ever been somewhere and your gut told you to leave? Then, you left and you woke up the next morning and found out something bad happened there. That is your spirit talking to you. Listen to your instincts and your spirit to guide you. When you have outgrown a city, relationship or job, recognize it. Have the faith to move on and start fresh.

Chapter 6
Fight

No matter who you are, we all have experienced heartbreak and pain. We must take steps to become innovative and rise above out bad circumstances in life. Being down and out has created some great champions and we rely on God the most when we are struggling in certain areas. When we open our eyes in the morning we have a chance to become better then we was yesterday. No matter what you are currently facing, or have faced in the past, you have the ability to rebuild, recover, revive and regroup. Yes fight! Fight for your health. Go to the gym, walk around the neighborhood, watch what you eat and stay away from Greasy foods. Some stuff you go through in life and you understand why it happened. Other stuff you go through you may not understand it.

Some stuff just comes out the blue and knocks you off your feet. Some challenges we face, we never expected to face them. You can work hard for your college degree and then come to find out you can't get a job. You got into some legal problems and now it's getting tough for you to take care of your family. I've been there; life can do you some unexpected challenges sometimes. One thing I learned is that feeling sorry for yourself and lying down all day will not change a thing. Get up throw the Kleenex away after you cried all night and come up with a plan of action that will improve your situation. Keep a positive attitude and come up with some creative ideas to improve business or whatever you want to achieve. In one moment of your life you may have sadness, heartbreak one turmoil. In another moment, you may experience joy, love, wealth and happiness. No matter what you are facing today determine in your heart that you will not let it break you. Decide in your life to use all the wisdom, skills and experiences from your life lessons. Consider it pure joy, whenever you face trials of many kinds, according to James 1:2 in the Bible.

It is important to remain optimistic when dealing with problems in your life. Worry and stress makes situations worse than what they actually are. Stress is a top reason for health problems, so it is important to keep your right frame of mind. You could be living life morally good and just going about minding your business. You don't bother people you just go to work and come home. All of a sudden you lose your job, you find out you have a serious health problem, someone you love dies or you get evicted. All kinds of different situations you can find yourself in, you are engulfed in a storm. Be strong and of good courage, do not fear nor be afraid of them; for the Lord your God, He is the One who goes with you. He will not leave you nor forsake you," says Deuteronomy 31:6 in the Bible.

Life's adversities can teach you things you need to know in this life. If you've never faced any problems in life you wouldn't know whether you're real, or not. One of the ways to tell if a diamond is real if you put it under intense pressure, it will produces a flawless diamond. Sometimes the problems in your life will build your prayer life. You will learn to depend on God for all the situations you encounter. We will encounter many failures throughout our life, it is important to not let the failures define us. You will see that failures can be overcome if we have faith. You can overcome any obstacle if you remain in faith and remain positive. You can't change yesterday no matter how hard you try. Yesterday is over, so leave it in the past.

There is a saying, "You can't cry over spilled milk." Whatever you are facing right now, do not let your mind go into a negative place. Sometimes going through failures in life can grow and humble us. When you are in your dark place in life, you're in the valley. Remain with a positive attitude and keep on trying and keep trying to make opportunities for yourself and your family. Your faith has to be stronger than your fears. You can't live your life in fear you have to have faith and fight. It would be wise to know God's word when things get difficult in your life. Knowing his word will keep your mind in perfect peace when you feel like losing your mind. What I learned about the bad times is that if you don't go through them, you will never be appreciative of the good one's. Life can be a series of unfortunate circumstances. Everyone is fighting a battle you know nothing about and everyone has had to make a comeback from some situation. You will be faced with adversity and struggle. You will not make wise decisions sometimes, if you remain humble and in faith, everything will be all right.

You cannot afford to live without hope and faith. Things that seem like they are hopeless are not always the case. When we feel outnumbered by our problem, remember to pray. In the Bible, he tells us in Psalms 91:11, "For he shall give his angels charge over thee, to keep thee in all thy ways." You can be down in the pits of life; you cannot know how you were going to make it. The thing to remember is to keep on trying. You will never realize how strong you are until you are faced with some great challenges. What you failed in yesterday is an experience that is already over with. Determine in your soul that every negative situation you encounter you will get wiser and better from it.

Life is not a straight line for myself and many other

people. It's filled with all kinds of problems, good times and bad times. One thing I learned is that what you focus on gets bigger. So, focus on your future goals and the things you want to achieve in your life. When times do not go as planned, just look at it as if the good Lord has something even better for you in store. It's easy to become discouraged by your situation, or the things you see. Your faith that things will get better must be stronger than your discouragement. You can think about a job or starting a business all day, unless you go put in an application for that job, unless you started doing some research on that business you want to start, you will never accomplish your goals unless you try. Life can be bruising at times, those unfortunate times can help us develop as a person.

Sometimes, you have to deal with people lying on your name at work, church and in the neighborhood. When problems happen in your life, you must face it with strength and power. You must be tough during adversity and rely on past life lessons and your faith to bring you through. When it's chaos all around, sometimes it's best to be still in times of confusion. It's hard to make good decisions when you are under stress, wait until you have a sound mind to make your move.

Chapter 7
Keep Your Mind Right And Take Action

We are going to have times where everything is going bad; our kids may be misbehaving or going down the wrong path, our marriage is in jeopardy and we are in and out of the hospital, and our mind is wondering if we are surviving in between.

In between those rough points keep your sense of humor and keep your faith. I wrote this book because I believe my experiences will help someone with hopes that they overcome the challenges they face. Whether you are behind bars, sick in the hospital or some other dark place in your life, you can restart and get your life back on track.

There is a lot of talent that is behind prison walls. Dedicate your life to staying out of trouble and do not go back to what got you in bondage in the 1st place. There is hope for any situation you encounter. I've been a school teacher in Texas for the last 6 years and one thing I am proud of is mentoring and guiding students to be successful in their life. As a teacher I not only advise students and nurtured them, I am also a good listener. I could relate to student struggles. Students, like many of us, need courage to overcome different struggles we are facing. You got to have perseverance and resilience in this life for the many storms you will find yourself engulfed in. Listen to your spirit; many times we have people around us that threaten our peace of mind and happiness. If we have people around who constantly threaten our happiness, even if it's family and friends, we must separate ourselves. We must let Faith have control over our lives in whatever situation we find ourselves. We must learn to develop faith over fear. The mind is powerful! When those negative thoughts come over your mind, rebuke it and get a fresh perspective. When the thoughts and things we do become bad, we must take control over our minds and form new and healthier habits.

Growing up in the hood, as I did, there are a lot of negative situations around you. You deal with police harassment, crime all around and people hating you for no reason. Now, don't get me wrong growing up in the hood you learn some valuable life lessons; if you did something wrong, the whole community would get on you about what you did. There is some good experiences growing up in the hood, there is also a lot of negative. We must throw out the self-hate and low thinking and raise our thinking during circumstances in life. A lot of people, especially African-Americans, have suffered greatly for many years. We have been hoping we would get reparations and/or that someone or something would help us with more happiness and opportunity. We as a people must be responsible for our own happiness and take action measures to improve our community and ourselves.

We are at a time in history where we can have a pity party and blame everyone else for our condition, or we can rise higher and have a joy and peace in our lives and neighborhoods. Young African-American men have so much to offer, the devil wants to destroy your life. However, the Lord gives you more than the devil does. This is a message to my drug dealing and gang banging brothers. You have to look at a situation like this, when you commit a crime you will be judged and sentenced by enemies. I know sometimes you don't even commit the crime, you get arrested anyway. In this world, we will have trouble we must search for peace and become innovators and creating the life we wish to have.

Be conscious of what you are doing with your time day-to-day. Try to be productive and set goals for yourself, short-term and long-term. To be where you would like to be in life you must have a personal career to achieve your potential. You will never be under perfect conditions; there will always be something going on. We must be bold and appointed in our actions toward life. Nothing comes to a sleeper, a dream. Get up and even if you don't have a job, go do some volunteer work and research on what it is you want to do. There is a saying, "we are a sum total of our actions." Make it up in your mind everyday that you have good actions to improve your current situation.

When we look around in our neighborhood at the condition of the community, we need a revival, not just in the buildings we see, in our hearts and minds as well. Some people you come into contact with on a daily basis look so sad and their conversations are extremely emotionally draining. When people have lost their joy for life and have a cold feeling toward others, or when we encounter people who are down in life, we must try to give them a word of encouragement. Tell them about a time you were down and the Lord answered your prayers and picked you right back up. We have to examine our minds and hearts and start having a love for one another. When life makes you want to break, we must develop a strong desire not to.

We must get back to the point where we laughed so hard we almost cried. We must slow down sometimes and listen to our senses and our spirit. Life is not to be weird or stressed over how you're going to make it from one day to the next. Nothing will be easy; you have to go through different battles and tests in life. At different times in life we will reach a point to where we want to improve our lives. We may be faced with different circumstances and situation that just make us want to do better. We must be faithful and pursue our goals and dreams with everything in us. Yeah we will go through struggles and hardships; one thing I learned about struggle and hardship is that it develops our character, strength and faith to move forward.

Blaming others for your mistakes or other misfortunes in life will do you no good. Taking responsibility for your actions and taking proactive steps to improve will help you tremendously. Complaining and nagging never accomplished a single thing. There are times in life when you fail or you don't succeed in a particular situation, rethink your plan. Re-organize and find a better way of handling your particular situation. Develop more knowledge and seek assistant. Sometimes in life we hit people that slow down. We face disappointment on the road of life, if we keep ticking eventually we will pass the speed bumps and hit the road again. No one can replace their past of different situations, we can start from today and do things better for the future. In life you must be dedicated, have perseverance and be persistent in whatever it is you want to achieve. It's important to be able to bounce back from many setbacks you will encounter in your journey in life.

We must take action every day that will improve

our emotional and physical well-being. When you are looking to improve your life it will take some courage and struggle. You have to separate your mind from certain situations to elevate. One thing I loved about the civil rights movement is even during all the oppression that blacks was facing you found hope and love.

Go back to school and start a new career; take a risk and if you're not being treated right in a relationship break off the affair. Travel and see the world, let go of your fear and have faith. Don't be a slave to the opinion of other people. Live your life freely and do the best you can do day-to-day. Get in a habit of feeding your spirit positive thoughts. For example, go to church and study the Bible to get in the Word. Cut off the gangster rap sometimes or some of those silly TV shows, because it is like junk food. Let your faith be stronger than your doubt, worry, fear and hang up. Many times we are the ultimate cause of our own happiness in life. Stop procrastinating and get in the game of life; don't put off what you could do today for tomorrow. Nothing will ever be perfect with time, in life we must live no matter what.

To improve in our lives and to make our community better, we must make better choices. Feel good about the direction of our lives and become confident in ourselves. What happened yesterday is in the past and we cannot change that, we can learn from it for the future. We have to throw out the window of self-doubt and self-loathing and become good role model for our neighborhoods and communities. Many times the pain we experienced yesterday is helping to stretch ourselves and grow how we never imagined. There is a saying, "no pain no gain." Many times when we are working out our bodies we feel pain, we endure the pain because we want a good-looking body or to achieve some fitness goal.

Even when we're sleepy, we get up early for work, take our kids to school and head to work. We will endure pain and discomfort to achieve what is right. We must fight to defeat the demons in our minds that hinder our greatness. Refuse to break your integrity when faced with hardship. Don't go out there and sell your body or drugs for a few bucks. Let us aim to be great men and women. I've been through a lot in my life and I admire other people who have been through a lot, are still surviving and thriving. Whatever we go through or whatever we are faced with we must develop a resilient spirit.

Chapter 8
Don't Let The Struggles Hold You Back

In life sometimes we will fail at certain things we get involved in. , we must not let fear hinder us in accomplishing our goals. Choose to be strong and bold over your fears. Feel the heat and do it anyway! You are stronger and wiser than you think you are. We have to put things in perspective in life. When we are faced with a difficult situation and are feeling fearful, we must manage our thoughts and/or overcome the fear. We must throw out of our minds the negative self-talk and the talk of critics. Nothing can be done about our past, to learn from it and look at it with courage. Be wary of people who are always negative, who is full of doubt, who keep drama and problems going, minimize your time around these people because they mean your mind no good.

Don't let other people's anxieties and fear stop you from being great and succeeding in life. Sometimes when I'm on Facebook it's so negative that you have to keep scrolling and avoid reading because it put such negativity into your spirit. We have to keep scrolling in real life around certain people because they are full of no good. We must have a discerning spirit with our family and friends. We can listen with a full heart, be careful about what we take in. You got to be wary of people who don't even go look for a job. Some people are just lazy and don't put any effort into trying to make their situation better. Some people want other people to take care of them and they have too much pride to work. Some people, even family, will be upset if you bring up work to them. They would be ready to fight and curse you out. There are people out there that have no purpose or desire to work. Some people will never find the heart to leave complacency; they have given up on living a life worth living.

If it was not for the struggles in life we would not appreciate the good times. Struggles in life teach us lessons and it humbles our spirits. Some stuff we would not appreciate if it was not for the struggles. When you work hard for your money, you appreciate it more than if it was just handed to you. Struggles mature your spirit and help you grow. So don't just run and coward down when you are faced with struggles. Face them with courage!

You may not know if you are real or not until you face some struggles. I wrote this book, Surviving in Between, because of the struggles and different circumstances I've encounter, as well as many others. Challenges will teach you wisdom that you would have never learned if everything were just easy going.

When trouble hits you or your home, or when you don't know how that court situation will turn out. You must have faith in the lord and in the power of his might. Be a person of action that accomplishes goals. No matter what you have been through in life, never give up. Instead, gain wisdom from each fight. Fighting will sharpen you with real world experience and you will gain knowledge that you never knew you had. Take pride in your struggle, help people who are struggling with similar things you have struggled with in the past and keep joy in your heart and mind.

We have life battles to fight, victories to cheer and a community to help. Keep your head up and stay strong and encouraged. Whenever you try to do good in the world, evil is present. There are some cruel people in this world and they will lie and say things about you that are not true. Never let the cruelness of the world take your happiness and sense of humor. We cannot let weak haters cause doubt or instill fear in our spirits that kill our goals and dreams. Whenever you sense worry in your life, sit still and think rationally. Calm yourself and if you're a person like myself, read some uplifting scriptures of the Word. Don't dwell over negative things that happened in the past.

Having anxiety over something you cannot control will do you no good. Every decision we encounter whether it's thinking about losing weight, changing locations or dumping the male we have been with for some time, will be stressful. Throw fear out the window and try your best to make wise decisions for your life. If we look over the shoulders of our life and look at what we survived yesterday, we would not be so concerned about what we will possibly face tomorrow. Many of us have endured some tough lessons yesterday and that should be more than enough to survive our current state. When negative thoughts or thoughts of fear enter your mind, we have the power to combat it with positive and uplifting thoughts. In life, it is important to have the right mindset. Once we practice having the right mindset we will win.

How does a kid learn to swim or ride a bicycle without being afraid of drowning or falling? The kid was once afraid to swim or ride a bike. As the kid practiced, the kid became unafraid. Once the kid faces the fears he once was afraid of, he will began to conquer them. When we take steps to face our fears we are forging ahead and we will come to see that what caused us fear is no longer dominant in our lives. Let's feed our faith over our fears and master our minds to develop a resilient spirit. You'll always have to deal with some hardships, be strong and wise in your actions.

To reach our full potential we must get up every

day with passion in our hearts to chase our goals and the things we want in life. We must stay motivated to achieve in life, even when things are not going our way. If you're waking up each day and your life is in shambles, it's time to wake up with a new life philosophy. Doubt, worry and fear diminishes your life because you will lack the confidence to move forward in your mind. Developing faith and having a positive mind state will help you better support your mental state. Each day, no matter what state you currently find yourself in, strategically plan your day and the direction you want to go in. Live a meaningful life; a life with goals and things that you want to accomplish. You can choose to be negative, around drama and gossip or you can choose to be positive in a way that increases your life value. We should live a life motivated to want to make things better for ourselves as well as our family. People that want a better body must be committed to going to the gym, working out and controlling what they eat. Whatever it is in life you want to achieve, you must be motivated to do so. You must have the faith and the desire to achieve your goals. If you don't believe in yourself nobody will, so with each day take the steps to get closer to your goals. Refocus and keep your dream alive by making yourself better and your community.

Don't let the distractions of the day steal your

motivation for accomplishing your goals. It's never a good idea to let the problems you are currently engulfed in make you lose your enthusiasm. Never become so distracted with the hassles of life that you lose focus on goals and things you want to accomplish. If married couples never put any real effort into sustaining their marriage, like not dating and doing stuff together or neglecting one another, then the marriage will be in trouble. You must keep your hope alive in whatever you're looking to accomplish, despite the setbacks you may encounter. Be bold toward your heart's desires. Take action, plan and do little steps each day until you reach your goals. When difficult situation come upon you in your life, take it with a smile, don't become bitter or angry knowing that you have the strength to face any challenge.

Keeping a good sense of humor and not letting the world make you bitter when things go wrong will help you in this life. When you hang around people who are doing negative things you will fall into the trap. You see it all the time, people in the wrong place at the wrong time and they get caught up in a mess. We should distance ourselves from drama and people who are up to no good. Live in the moment, go outside and feel the weather. Take time to listen to people and give encouraging advice, if you can. Don't be so bogged down in your mind that you miss the beauty of life. Take stock in the beauty that is around you.

As you go about living day-to-day, take stock into your emotions and the emotions of people we come into contact with on a daily basis. Don't live in yesterday or the tomorrow. Be motivated to live in the now and focus our minds on being the best. A lot of people live in yesterday and blame it for their current state in life. You see it everyday in our neighborhoods. Every time you see certain people, they talk about what they did in high school, many years ago. They talk about how much money they use to have; their minds is stuck in yesterday. If you ask them what they are doing today in the present, their minds go blank. They don't want to take responsibility for their lives today and don't want to take actions to improve it. These individuals have become unproductive in their life and memory is hindering them from moving forward tomorrow.

Let's take this guy, for example, who is 30 years of age, still blames his parents for how his life has turned out. The kid who is now an adult is not taking any responsibility for his life and is just wallowing in self-pity. The people who blame their parents are the people who always live in yesterday and need a renewing in their mind. They need a new mental discipline that will allow them to be productive, successful citizens today.

God can pick nobodies and make them somebodies without consulting anyone. Yes, you have to believe and have faith that you can overcome. Look out the backdoor of your life and look at the challenges you already survived and the things you already overcame.

Become alive again and find your step once more. Get that love in your heart; find that happiness again. Looking back on yesterday and smiling at the good times should make you happy on the inside. Don't let yesterday prevent you from doing good things or creating great memories. Don't be bitter about things that happened years ago, its over, let it go and move on. Dwelling on past hurts will just leave your spirit down. You meet some women and they're still talking about the guy whom did them wrong 15 years ago. Once you start talking to them, you realize they think everyone is the same and they are still bitter about it and in an emotional bondage. Baby girl, you're not going to ever grow unless you put the problems of yesterday in your mind of forgetfulness. Don't let the situations of yesterday steal your joy for today.

Sometimes at night we can't sleep because we thinking about that court date, doctor's appointment or some other situation. Whenever you get to those nights and cannot sleep, pray and meditate on your particular situation. Ask yourself, what steps can I take today to make my life better?

Don't avoid the hardships that life puts in front of you, conquer them all with faith. In life, you are not the only one going through ups and downs. When we face our tough time head on, we learn to grow through the difficult situations. Protect your peace. Get rid of toxicity, cleanse your space and cultivate love. Limit the amount of negativity in your space. Some people are always negative and are not a joy to be around. Limit your interactions with these toxic people; it will save you some peace of mind. We must limit the amount of gangster rap music and start listening to some uplifting music from time to time. Also, protect your mind from the scandals and drama you encounter. Be conscious of the information you absorb. Move your life forward with empowering and positive information. Be proactive in life; don't wait until everything is perfect to start marching toward your goals and desires. Observe the small details of life. Ask yourself, am I being too mean to my kids? Am I on the phone too much when I should be listening? Do I listen intently to what people are saying and give sound advice? You should live and be active; take a walk around the park for about 20 minutes each day. Go workout, play a sport or hobby you enjoy. Take a trip to the museum, the mountains or somewhere. Challenge negative thoughts that come into your mind. Look at the situation in a different light. Talk to a friend that you trust. Develop a balanced perspective of situations you are dealing with in life.

Chapter 9
Taking Charge And Making Plans

Take charge of your lifestyle, thoughts, emotions and the way you deal with problems. Nothing kills goals more than procrastinating. So, get to moving. Set aside time for yourself and recharge your spirit. If you are walking through the valley of despair keep walking. So many people give up when they are walking through the valley of despair, if you keep walking and don't give up there will be happiness on the other side. Pick up your head; regain your zeal for life. Look at how far you have come and how much you have overcome. Just looking back at yesterday should give you strength for the fight for tomorrow. Don't waste your days doing nothing, set some goals. You cannot expect good things to happen if you never go out and try stuff. Time goes fast; one day we look up and we're 25, then we're 30 and now we're 35 and it seems like life is passing us by. Don't spend your days squandering your time. Starting today, lets make a vow to live our life with aim and being proactive each day to be productive. Regain your focus in life and stop wandering through life like the lost sheep. Have a purpose in life even if it's for your kids. Look for ways each and every day to progress, whether it is going to community college part-time while you're working, or whatever, just make sure you have a plan for advancement.

Life can burden you down. Sometimes, you don't know which way to turn or which way to go. Take a deep breath, go walk around the park or go volunteer at a homeless shelter. Do good things that will make you feel alive.

Instead of being overwhelmed by burdens, have faith and believe that when you plant good seeds that you are going to be overwhelmed by Jesus' blessings. That's why I say fight for your happiness, your joy and/or your marriage, never give up or give in.

Many people today suffer silently. You talk to them and they don't tell you what's wrong, you know something is wrong. There is sadness with the way their life has turned. I want to encourage you today if you are suffering from sadness to get your life back. Examine yourself; ask yourself what steps could you take to be a happier person? Am I being nice and respectful to people? Do I want to go back to school and pursue that career? What short-term goals do I want to accomplish? Where do I see myself 5 years from now? Ask yourself the tough questions and come up with steps to improve your life. Technology, Facebook and Instagram is ok, could you be using your time more productively. Could you limit your time on social media to go help some kids with homework by volunteering? Looks for a job or spend time with and elderly person. Life can knock you out of focus if you are not careful. Let's vow to make our attitudes better than they were yesterday. Create a vision for your life, no matter what you have been through, no matter how old you are, create a vision for your life. Sometimes you have to look in the mirror and ask yourself, what has my life become?

If you don't like where you currently are in your life, you must take bold steps to improve. A young man went to college and got his Bachelor's degree in finance. Then, he went on to get his Master's degree. The young man became a school teacher for 6 years and it looked like things were going well in his life. The young man was even an insurance agent for 6 years. Then he made some unwise decisions in his insurance business and was hit with some legal problems.

It doesn't matter where you are currently at in life, you can make a change. Having a degree doesn't mean you will have success. There are homeless people with Master's degrees. The thing with life is you must stay prayerful and learn from your mistakes. You don't know what turns life could give you, if you're turning on the wrong street you must make a U-turn. Live each day to the best of your ability and make your days count. Don't just sit away and idle away your time. Set goals, have courage, move from one thing to the next, knowing that you are learning from each and every time you encounter difficult situations. Everybody will not be happy for you when you recognize things need to change around you. You can't live a life where you are constantly trying to please everyone and leaving your happiness unchecked. With the demands of life each and every day it is important to say no sometimes.

Even with our kids, once they become a certain age, we need to say no to them so they can become self-reliant. You never want your child to be 30, 35 or 40 years old still living off of another person, or me. Saying no to your kids early on and making them do chores for their work will help the kids later in life. This is the same thing as with the family or anything else we want to accomplish. Living life when you just going about your life and then, boom! You find yourself in a storm. Sometimes the storm can be in our minds with worrying and negative thoughts. Negative thoughts many times come out of nowhere, like a crash you did not see coming. That's how quickly negative thoughts pour into our minds. However, when negative presents itself in our minds, we don't have to let it live in our minds. We have power and we must use our power to cast down on those negative thoughts that enter our minds. We have the power to erase those negative thoughts by meditating on the Word of God. When we speak the word out our minds, the thoughts will come into arrangement with what we are speaking.

Fight. I love that word! Fight the enemy in your mind by meditating and speaking positive words over your life and family life.

When those thoughts come into your mind, cast them away immediately. Be intentional about your joy and gaining happiness. Intentionally fill your mind and your heart with good positive thoughts of the Lord's blessing over your life. Our thoughts are powerful, that's why always listening to gangsta rap music is not good. Mix it up sometimes; listen to some gospel or some uplifting music.

Our thoughts are powerful and whatever you believe in, your heart will achieve. Have thoughts on good uplifting things, and do positive things with your life. Your thoughts if they are not challenged will have you fearful and insecure. You can hinder your own progress in life if your thoughts are not correct. Make it up in your mind from this day forth that you will have good uplifting thoughts. Your own worse enemy sometimes is the person that is staring back at you in the mirror. When you have poor thoughts and think lowly of yourself, you yourself will not realize how valuable you are and hinder your future. When you look yourself in the mirror each and every day, be proud of who you are and have the courage to move forward. Don't let the negative voices in your mind win; don't let fear and negative thoughts win. Declare this is a new day and I will be better than I was yesterday. Doubt and disbelief hits us all at times, if you can have faith and keep your mind and spirit up you can conquer your doubt.

When at those times at night where you can't sleep and you're stressing about tomorrow. Stress will do you no good. What would do you good is meditating and praying over the issue that is bothering you. Free yourself from self-oppression, free yourself in your mind. Get rid of negative thoughts, people and environments that hold you back in life. If you know that you are trying to improve your life don't even go around people who are bad and drama filled. You know certain people that just do bad stuff and never have any peace. Limit yourself to those people because they are not good for your growth.

When life is bad and it seems like your life is on a downward spiral, it could be the Lord's way of speaking to you. Sometimes you will wake up in the mornings and say to yourself, "My life is a mess." When you are going through those rough patches, it is important to meditate and pray. Instead of complaining about our struggles and things we are facing, look at your problems through the eyes of faith, you will realize you gained more wisdom and faith through your hardships. Many times the hardships of life develops you in ways that if you would not have went through anything you would not have that deeper understanding of life. The hardships of life will humble you and give you the confidence you need to withstand. The testing of our faith matures us, produces perseverance and grows our faith stronger.

Chapter 10
Control Your Surrounds

We will not understand everything that happens in our life, if you remain positive through it all you will come out a better person. When people lie on you or you are facing trials, it is important not to become bitter and filled with hate. Keep your humor, stay positivity and have faith. Stay around positive people because hanging around miserable, unhappy people is bad for your spirit. Learn to strive for peace no matter what comes your way or what situation you may encounter. At your workplace, when everybody else is gossiping and keep the drama stirred up, remain at peace and fill the atmosphere with your peace-filled actions. Inner peace does not come from our circumstances, from what we do, the people we love or from those who love us. Inner peace is the blessed assurance of God's unfailing presence with us at all time and in every situation. Inner peace resides within our souls and we can always tap into that place of serenity and tranquility. Even in the midst of a storm. Pease is not the absence of chaos, it is the presence of the Lord in the midst of all hell breaking loose.

Make it your aim to gain happiness and put away those things that would make us less than. Take risks in life and connect with others in love. Set high goals for yourself and have faith you can hit your goals. Feed your own faith; let your doubt starve to death. No matter what giants you are facing today in life, calm yourself and take control of your thoughts and actions.

You may be surviving some bad situations life has dealt you, survive. The wind may have come and took your breath away, get back up and fight. Some things happen in life where you will have no choice to have faith. If you don't have faith you will worry yourself into a coma or you will not gain the strength needed to take the required risk. When you lack faith, doubt will come into our minds when we are striving for greatness or trying to make improvements in our lives. Whenever you are ambitious and attempting to become magnificent, doubt will be in our minds singing a sad song. Be protective over your thoughts and rebuke the negativity that would try to invade your mind. When I started working on this book, surviving in between things was popping in my mind like you wasting your time on this book, what if nobody cares to read it. I told myself even if this book helps just one person, it was well worth the effort. We cannot progress in life if we constantly let self-doubt win. We have to have faith in our capabilities, whether its starting a business or going to law school, whatever you want to accomplish you must not let the doubts that pop up in your mind win. When we struggle and we keep on striving despite obstacles in our path we gain from it the tenacity to win. Lots of people give up on their dreams because of the road travelled. The people who see their goals and dreams come to past are the people who keep fighting and never give up.

Life will not always be good; there will be some valleys and trials to endure. Having a good attitude and keeping your sense of humor when things are not going as planned is key. When you have faith, things can turn around. I love rap music, when I am going through a storm I can't listen all that non-sense. I have to listen to gospel music; I have to listen to some uplifting music. In those times, I have to get around people who are talking and speaking positive faith. If you take an inventory over your life and look back at what all you've been through, look at what you accomplished yesterday when faced with obstacles in your path. Your mental toughness allowed you to beat the odds.

Faith is an action. Even when all the odds are stacked against you, when you are dealing with frustration and disappointment, faith will have us hopeful even when the natural things don't look good. Faith is an action, even though the road we're traveling may be dark with a lot of speed bumps and we really can't see. With faith, we will make it to our destination. There will never be perfect conditions in our lives to begin with. Whether you want to start that business or get married and have a family. Whether you want to finish school, there will always be something. Begin anyways, because the sooner you begin the closer to your goal you will be. The graveyard is full of men and women who missed their moment because of doubt and inaction.

We must be the masters of our fate. We must take decisive action in our lives each and every day. A lot of us have been through a lot; yesterday is filled with pain and some bad memories. Yesterday we were unforgiving and bitter toward some people whom we think wronged us. Let's make the decision to let go of the misery of yesterday. Let go of every thought that is not beneficial or holding you back in your mind. Let the Lord work on your spirit, mediate and pray for newness. Learn from yesterday, let it make you better, don't dwell on yesterday. Focus on tomorrow, the things you want to accomplish and loved ones you want to spend time with. Being a person of faith does not mean life will be easy and you won't encounter trials. What being a person of faith means is that whatever situation one may find himself in; the person will let their faith overcome their fear. When you have faith you can find the sunshine in the midst of rain. Let's make it up in our minds to overcome our doubt and fear. Let's focus our minds on advancement and progressing in life. If you are one of my friends reading this book from prison, lets focus on coming home. Make a plan and vow to the Lord that when you get home you will leave crime and bad influences alone. Make it up in your mind that you will be a productive citizen.

Let's fight for our children, let's fight for our loved ones, let's fight for our community. You have been equipped to live a great life. Strive daily to be a person of action. Don't just waste your time doing nothing on a daily basis. There is much you could be doing. When we look at circumstances that we face from time to time, they will either defeat us or develop us. When we look at things in the natural, we can perceive that everything is falling apart and we begin to speak and to operate from a defeated state of mind. If we shift our perception to view it by faith from a spiritual perspective, it will cause us to be mindful of our position of victory and we will see that things are being divinely reconstructed to allow our circumstances to line up and allow us to be prepared and positioned to fulfill a divine purpose. Develop the mindset to win and succeed in life. Take risks, come up with action plans to improve your situation. When your thinking is not in good shape, you limit the success you could be having. Many times to reach our full potential we must stretch ourselves. If your reality is not a good reality currently, take aggressive steps toward shaping your future for a better tomorrow. Our circumstances that we currently find ourselves in are not permanent. Shake off the self-pity and start believing again. Sometimes the road of life can be filled with many difficulties and trials. The Lord can use our trials for his glory.

The Lord can use our trials for the sake of transforming others somewhere down the line that are facing hardships. Take initiative over your life, you can live in a nice house and take care of your family. Learn a new trade, enroll into school and go to network meetings. Your dreams can become your reality, if you don't give up. Never allow yourself to become so intently focused on or intimidated by what seems to be an overwhelming task at hand that you fail to see and tap into the potential that you have within you to resolve whatever comes your way. You have what it takes to rise above and overtake the thing that is trying to overwhelm you. You are an overcomer. Look back on your life through the backdoor of it. The time is over for trying to wait for someone to try to come and save us from our condition. The time is over for trying to wait for the perfect conditions in our lives. We must move now with faith and courage, while we chase down our goals and dreams. We must become more self-reliant in the days ahead. When different struggles of various sorts hits you in life, don't get discouraged. Many times we learn more from the struggle than we could ever imagine. Struggle is necessary to develop our character and many times the struggle will bring out our creativity. Let's take bold steps to becoming great in order to achieve our dreams. Develop drive; be ambitious toward things you want to achieve in life.

No matter what your current circumstance is right now, it is only temporary. You can bounce back from any setback that is placed in your path. Be proactive each and every day to bring those things you imagined for yourself and loved ones to fruition. You can be in the fail house right now, or you could even be living in the ghetto. You must have a vision that is greater than your reality. Ride through some nice neighborhoods every now and then. Vision can help you overcome your current circumstance. With faith and vision, hard work will bare fruits if you never give up. We can't always see the twists and turns life will deal us, we must see the good in every situation and learn from every mistake. You have the power to shape your life into a life that will bring you joy. Take inventory of your conversation and the words you are speaking daily to yourself or to other people. Make it up in your mind to speak only of positive things. Refrain from engaging in negative self-talk or negative talk with other people. Set big goals for yourself; there is an old saying shoot for the stars even if you miss you will be at the top. Don't settle for poverty when your potential is much greater. Everyone has been through some stuff in life; some people have gone through more than others. Whatever you went through, stop crying about it, the world doesn't care and will not feel sorry for you. Get up, dry your tears and fight with everything in you. You are responsible for your life at the end of the day and you must know and have faith that you can change your reality.

Write down or put into your phone 10 steps you can take to improve your life. You want to live a life in which you know your spirit is fulfilled. We know when we are living beneath our means. So when you know that you are living below where you are capable, we must take steps to improve. Sometimes I am riding with my son in the car and he always asks me, "Daddy where are we going?" Sometimes I tell him where we're going, sometimes I don't. In the times I don't tell him, I surprise him and take him to the park or something. Many times in this ride of life we don't know exactly where we are going, if you have faith and keep a positive attitude, the Father has some surprises for you. Take that leap of faith even though you don't know exactly how it will turn out. One thing is for sure, if you never take the leap you will always be on the bench, not knowing how far you could have gone. In life you learn from trial and error. None of us will ever be perfect. There will never be perfect conditions, without mistakes you will never gain total progress. Take action each and every day to advance your current situation. Failures in life can make you better. Failures can humble you and you learn wisdom from your failures. Many successful people have failed at numerous things in life. The key was they never gave up. Dust off your failures. Yesterday is over. Begin again. If you just sit at the house all day doing nothing, the chances that you would be unhappy would be great.

So don't just sit around all day being non-productive. Get into the game of life and live a life full of actions. When traveling on a train and that train goes through a tunnel, you are surrounded by darkness you don't let fear of the unknown cause you to jump off the train because of that. Instead, you sit still and you trust that the engineer of that train will get you through the dark place, back into the light and safely to our destination. So no matter how dark life's situation may seem to be at times, we can trust the engineer of our life is leading us and believe without a doubt that he will bring us safely through the darkness and into the light. In life you cannot depend on people to take care of you. You must take control of your own life and be responsible for your own happiness. Many times when you are making moves in life you will be your own cheerleader. Sometimes the road will get hard and you must encourage yourself. Act on your goals and use your time wisely to advance from the current state you find yourself in. Advancing is not all about money either. Some of us need to advance spiritually and emotionally. You see or hear on the news every day of someone that was well off financially, blowing his or her brains out. Money doesn't solve all problems and we all need progress in some areas of our lives. Things will not just come to you. You must act on the things that you want. There have been many cases where people started from nothing and now have built up their businesses and are now worth millions.

Develop a mindset that you will win come hell or high water. Develop a mindset of action that you will work towards your goals and dreams. There have been stories where you had men and women in prison. They came home, went to law school and became lawyers. There have been people who have been through a lot in life and they fought their way out of their circumstance. The people who started from nothing and had many challenges had faith and they acted on their faith. Lacking morals and courage is more damaging than lacking wealth. We will make mistakes and go through some desperation moments. Sometimes we will lack good morals and integrity, if you learn from your mistakes, you can begin again. When you get your mind strong and develop good character, happiness is just around the corner. In life you must crawl before you can walk. Many times it is a great struggle before progress. Don't complain about the struggle, many times the struggle is building your character. Sometimes we feel like we are going through hell and we just want to give up. We must remember that strength and faith is developed in our struggles. Fiery trials are used to burn away that which is not beneficial to our betterment. We can't give up and allow the hellish situation to cause us to walk away and not get our promised blessing. We must keep holding on and be bold with our actions. We must become intentional with our time and keep pressing through. Don't let cynicism and pessimism kill your hopes and dreams for tomorrow.

When you encounter people who are down and out, don't become down and out with them instead give them an encouraging word. We all have potential to become great, don't let negative stuff invade your mind and your spirit to where you lose your will and you become another negative person. Rise above the negativity and set high goals for your life. Rekindle your joy for living, help others while you are going on about your life, cast down your doubts and rekindle that faith. Some people when they call, you should not even pick up the phone. Every time they call involves some drama or problems. These people are energy vampires and if you are not careful will suck your joy right out of you. Take inventory of the things you say from day to day and watch what people say to you. Some conversations aren't even worth engaging in because it is not cultivating positivity. Yesterday and its unfulfilled duties and desires are gone. Today is a new day filled with new mercies and a fresh supply of hope. So no matter what may have gone on or gone wrong yesterday, forget about it and let it go. Each new day begins with a choice. We can choose to stress and worry about what lies ahead or we can choose to enter into the day with the mindset that no matter what comes our way, it is all in the Lord's hands and he will work things out for our ultimate good. Although we cannot control the things we have to deal with from day to day, we can control out attitude towards it.

We can choose to speak of the good things. We can choose to remain at peace. We can choose to deal with every situation with a loving and patient attitude. We must maintain our happiness even when things around us will tell us otherwise. There will be pain, hardship and injustice we will face if we remain calm and have faith, things will work out. Never abandon your hope for the future and always keep your mind protected from poison. Even amidst the darkest of our day, is a beacon of light. Let people know that joy and charisma exists. That may be the hope that someone needs to not give up. Your mother and father may have been on crack. You may have grown up around poverty. Your home life may have not been ideal you can develop a thankful spirit. Choose happiness even when the world seems angry and mad. When you're in traffic and people are flying, trying to get past you, let them go. Pullover in the other lane. Don't blow your horn at people, be nice to everyone you never know what someone is dealing with. When people come to you talking that victim talk, you can listen and don't have to be rude, instead be a person of faith talk. Just like a kid that is with his/her parents, the kid is happy with small things like going to the park. Be a person of joy and take pleasure in where you are currently at in life and be appreciative. Become joyful in meeting life's demands and take steps to stretch yourself beyond your comfort zone. No matter what challenges, troubles or struggles you faced yesterday, don't let that be your focus as you begin tomorrow.

Purposely focus on everything good and be conscious of the words you speak daily. Celebrate the victories be thankful for the growth you have experienced. Acknowledge the many blessings and the things you have accomplished in spite of the hardships you've had to endure. You are in control of your life at the end of the day. Lay down and cry tonight if you have to when you are done crying, put some action plans down or steps you will take to succeed. Your emotional state is a choice. There are things you could do each and every day to create joy in your life. Many people in their darkest hours, they feel they may need to break their integrity or compromise who they are. Many people become desperate when they are broke and end up doing something foolish. Don't cave in to the impulses to cheat or do something you'll regret. There are many of my brothers in prison because they acted on their impulses and neglected what they knew was the right thing to do. We must learn from our mistakes as well as other people's mistakes. Maintaining good morals and character will go a long way. Everyone has made mistakes and felt their fair share of disappointment. We can learn from our disappointments yesterday and use them to help us grow in the future. The world needs to hear good voices. When we see evil present, we should speak out against it. Stay away from gossip and ridicule. Don't become so easily offended. We have to get back to that love we used to have for one another and develop good character.

Your thoughts your actions become your character. That's why it is important to fill your mind with the word of God and surround your mind with good thoughts sometimes. There are enough negative thoughts that hit our mind from people we talk to, to the music we listen to. So make it a goal of yours to fill your thought pattern with good, positive thoughts. When you do good things in life you feel better about yourself. When you do evil things in life you become regretful over past mistakes. So let's make it up in our mind today, no matter where you are reading this book or your current stage in life, let's live a life of sowing good seeds. Let's vow to make decisions and actions to become good model citizens. When things around you are filled with anger and people around you are frustrated, be the stable and solid person who is not easily offended. Let's concentrate on ensuring that our communities are safe. Let's work on things that will bring us joy and fulfillment. In everything we do, every small detail, let us think it out carefully. Let's make it a goal to respect one another. We all have had different walks in life. We never know what people are going through and have been through, so let's make it a goal to love and respect each person we come into contact with. Whatever your desire is in life, whether it's your career, love life, whatever you want you must first put action towards it. If you fail to put action toward your goals, regret will follow you. If you are in poverty and you just waste your time each and every day looking for a handout your chances of staying in poverty will be great.

When you are at those stages in life where you find yourself frustrated and become impatient, it is important to calm yourself down so you will not make a decision you will regret. Many of us get ourselves into the worst mess because we lack patience. When we don't have enough money, we will do something that we regret if we are not careful. When you are not patient, you will give up on that person too soon or that business. So from this day forward let's be patient with the things in life so that we will not compromise our integrity. At any given moment we have two options: to step forward into growth or to step back into safety. When I had my insurance business, I was struggling, and I was disappointed I was not progressing like I should. So in the desperation for money I lacked integrity and morals. Many times we will break our morals and integrity because things don't turn out like we would like and we get ourselves in a world of trouble. Whether you're running a business, working out trying to lose weight, don't give up or stop because results are not coming as fast as you would like. Keep working hard to achieve great results. Disappointment will hit us all, do not let it break your spirit. Begin again. Don't let the mistakes of yesterday keep you from striving for greatness for tomorrow. Learn through your disappointment to come up with new goals and aims. Stop calling those things that are right now as if they will always be that way. Use your words and actions to bless your future. Stop speaking what you see and starting speaking what you seek. Stop speaking how you feel, start speaking faith.

When you are desperate, you will not be wise in your decision-making. You see beautiful women walking the streets selling their bodies because they have become desperate. There are millions of people in prisons around the United States for various charges because they became desperate for money. When you are desperate you are tempted to break integrity. We have all made some unwise decisions when we lacked. Many times when you are in need you are not even thinking about your actions will affect yourself or your family. In life you can suffer bad breaks and get knocked down from time to time. Life has a way of humbling you where you will not look down on people look for ways to help. In those desperate times, keep your integrity and when you meditate and have faith, your situation can turn around. As we keep our focus on our creator by meditating on his word and not dwelling on what is going on in the world or the things that may be going wrong around us, we are not so quick to panic, stress or get desperate. Things in this life will never be perfect when our focus is on the Lord it can always be peace filled. No good comes from being angry and bitter. You control your emotions; don't let others control your emotions. Doubt sees the obstacles, faith sees the way. Doubt sees the darkest night, faith sees the light of day. Doubt dreads taking a step, faith steps out and soars on high. Doubt always questions and always has to see, with hope and confidence, faith boldly declares I believe even though I cannot see.

Refuse to allow doubt to rob you of the victory faith has in store for you. Be a person who uplifts people and watch the words you speak daily. Monitor your conversations and if the conversation is going negative, ease your way out of conversation. Don't practice it being a habit getting caught up in drama and speaking negative. Make it a habit of speaking life. Develop actions each and every day that your kids, family, community will be proud of. We will face giants sometimes living day to day, be a person of good integrity and you will win every time. Don't give up on yourself, fight to make improvements daily. Choose to fix your mind on good things. Make choices that will cause you to continuously keep good thoughts. As you do, your mind will be filled with peace and day-by-day you will start gaining victories. Let's regain that love that we once had in our hearts for one another. Don't let the world turn you into a loveless and heartless person. Life is short. Despite yesterday's mistakes or today's pain we must love more deeply. The enemy likes to get us to focus on the negative and always view our lives from our negative experiences. We have to be mindful of what we meditate on and refuse to get caught up focusing on the negative. Focus on what we know to be God's track record of goodness to us and his love for us. Continuously reminding ourselves of our many blessings and how God has sustained us through every difficult and every uncertain situation. And how he has provided for us time and time again. The more we focus on the Lord and the good, the more we will see how the good definitely outweighs the bad.

Don't build your wall up so much in your life that you block out blessings and love from others. Don't let the past hurt of life rip away your joy, happiness and connections with others. If you are a person who cannot get over yesterday's hurt and pain. If so, you are choosing to let the hurts of yesterday rob you from the joy of tomorrow. Times of shaking and uncertainty will come. Life's events will be tossed around and everything we thought we could count on seems no longer dependable. The shaking in our lives can help us grow and reach our full potential. When life seems to be coming apart at the seams, we must remind ourselves of God's sovereignty and realize that the more we draw near to him, he will keep us from falling apart. Many things in our life happen to us and we are involved in many different storms. No matter what happened yesterday you are still here. No matter what situation you currently find yourself involved in, you are still capable and powerful. You are not your circumstance. Many storms in life happened to you you survived and made it through. You can use any bad circumstance and it could be used for your advantage. You learn many lessons while you are going through the storms of life. You learn wisdom, what to do and what not to do. Life is the best teacher. You are still fully equipped with every single tool you need to fulfill your purpose. Many times you survived hardships in life is because the fire inside you burned brighter than the fire around you. When you go through storms in life and when you make it over you develop an appreciation for life.

Don't dig up in doubt what you have planted in faith. Keep fighting, keep learning, and keep growing. If you don't give up, what you planted in faith will happen. Even though there are days I know you wish you could change about the past. There is a reason the rearview mirror is so small, and the windshield is so big, focus on what goals you want to accomplish, focus on the things you can do today to improve your present circumstance if you not happy. The windshield is much bigger because where you headed is much more important than what you left behind yesterday.

Instead of being overwhelmed by your burdens, just believe that you are going to be overwhelmed by blessings. A lot of times I use my GPS to get basically everywhere I go. Sometimes I take a wrong route or I pass up the street I was supposed to turn on. When I make those mistakes while driving, the GPS will reroute me to get back on the right track. Sometimes in life we get off track and we are confused on which way to turn. Just like the GPS if we keep our faith, we can be rerouted when we take the wrong turn or get off track. In life with people that you come into contact with on a daily basis, you never know what they are going through. Make it a habit of always being kind and nice to people. That one encouraging word or smile can make a huge difference in the life of someone who is on the verge of giving up. Refuse to let frustration or an unpleasant situation dictates your response to fulfill your purpose.

When an issue arises in our lives, we are quick to speak what is on our mind and usually what's on our mind in that moment is rooted in doubt, fear, disbelief and worry. Remind yourself to stop being so quick to speak what's in your head. Take a moment to reflect before you speak. As we live, we serve as examples for people who watch us when we don't realize they are watching us. When you have a good heart and you make efforts to make things better for yourself and your community, people will be inspired by your story.

We all make mistakes and we sometimes wish we could do things over. We can learn valuable lessons from our mistakes and the pain we felt yesterday could be inspiration to fuel tomorrow. Each new day begins with a choice. We can choose to stress and worry about tomorrow or we can choose to enter into the day with the mindset that no matter what comes our way, the Lord is in control and he will work things out for our good. We cannot control the things that we have to deal with from day-to-day, we can control our attitudes toward it. We can choose to speak of the good things. We can choose to remain at peace. We can choose to deal with every situation with a loving and patient attitude. Develop big visions for your life. You hear stories everyday of people overcoming great odds to become a success. Make daily efforts to improve your life. Don't just sit around all day, doing nothing and being non-productive. Hold yourself to a high standard and become disciplined with your time. Don't just waste it away doing nothing.

There are many volunteer organizations that need help. There are many wayward teens that need a word of encouragement. Find a cause that is important and there you will find many ways to help. We must develop good morals and act with integrity in all of our dealings. Back in the day when I was a child, and I did something wrong, it was nothing for someone in the community to jack me up. We can't focus on trying to be our kid's friends, kids need good parents who will guide them in the right direction.

We must call wrong out whether it is at our job, in the community or in our homes. Wherever you are in life, don't become complacent and get to the point you don't care what goes on in the home, job or community. Some of us face so many challenges in life that we don't think we can inspire others. When you tell your story and about how you overcame you are inspiring others. Wake up each day fight to improve your tomorrow. Be proactive in learning new skills and challenge yourself to grow mentally, emotionally and spiritually. Many of us are creative and we all have different gifts. Use your gifts to uplift your community and world. Some of our communities have become a challenge for us to live in for various reasons. We could go on and on about the reasons some of our communities are a mess. We must ask ourselves, what can I do to make my life and community a better place? Are we speaking with young men and telling them that killing your own is genocide?

Are we speaking with them about the devastating effects of selling drugs and what could happen to them? These are questions not just for the urban areas the suburbs as well. Let's ask ourselves the tough questions to improve our lives as well as the lives of those people around our community and us. You must act with integrity in all of your dealings. We must learn from mistakes and we must not fear becoming unpopular when doing what is morally just. No matter what circumstance you find yourself in, always maintain integrity. Take responsibility for your actions and don't blame others for your failures. In reading this book let's come up with an action plan to improve our communities and ourselves. Let's start a movement, a revolution in our lives and in our communities for the better. Drugs in the inner city have sent many young black men to prison for decades. The prison situation is a whole different topic.

My brothers, we must stop killing each other and regain that love for each other we once had. Not just the black community also all communities suffer in one form or another. We can rise above our shortcomings if we have faith and we are committed to contributing in ways that make us better. Whatever situation you currently find yourself in you do have the power to become great. One wrote this book to challenge and inspire and to encourage you to act with wisdom. You have some people out here that blame society, their parents and anybody else for their poor choices. When you don't stand up and take responsibility then you end up living a mediocre life, suffering from your bad choices.

Do you realize when you are shooting your brother or selling your drugs the whole community suffers including yourself in the long run? No matter what past you may have had, whether you raised yourself or had help, you are responsible for your own life. To help some people, you must be direct and truthful if you want them to improve. You have some men who don't even for look for a job; they just live off their family and women. Some of these men if you try to correct them will be ready to fight you. We must always be direct even if it hurts in telling people what is good for them. We must do the very best we can each and every day and we must ask the good Lord for wisdom in decision-making. It is not wise to hand around lazy people, drama people, people who engage in negative behaviors. We don't have to judge people and we don't have to let them around us.

Choose to be around positive, uplifting people. We have no time for mediocrity. We live in an era now where there is a bunch of talking little action. We as a community must move from words and come up with some thoughtful solid actual efforts to help the community. We all must respect each other's opinions because we all come from different walks of life. Let us develop the discipline for greatness and let us wake up each day with goals for the day and things we wish to accomplish. Be proactive with your life each day. Whether it is going to the gym and working out, starting a new business or looking for a job. Come up with a list of action steps you can take each day to reach your goals.

We must develop that spirit that the leaders of the 60's left us. Leaders such as Martin and Malcolm had different strategies for achieving goals both men's actions were to make a difference in the lives of Blacks in America. They fought to improve the lives of their families and the communities around the world. There is so much drama in the community, one thing we have to remember, those of us who are looking to make a difference is that we are all fighting together trying to make situations better. Let us work hard toward unity in the community.

Back during the 60's the people worked together, stayed together, cried together and overcame together. If we are going to achieve and uplift our communities, we must get back to that unity and love. We must be honest in our dealings with each other and people that we come into contact with on a daily basis. In life you can find yourself in a world of trouble if you are not honest in your dealings. Let's make a commitment to ourselves and our community to be honest in all situations we encounter. We must learn from our mistakes and take responsibility for our actions. Learn from your mistakes; don't repeat the same mistakes over and over again. Be responsible for yourself and your family. You can't blame people for your downfalls in life you can take corrective actions to right your wrongs and get back up on your feet again. Learn from other people's mistakes and use wisdom in your dealings.

If something sounds too good to be true, use caution and wisdom in dealings. Be respectful of everyone that you meet. You never know what battles someone is dealing with. Your kindness, smile, could change their whole outlook on their situation. Strive each and every day to be good to our fellow men and ourselves. Ask yourself, what can I do today to make my world and my community a better place? Let's strive to become good men and women of good character. Let us live a life where we have a good conscience when we go lay down at night. Let's aspire to make our ancestors proud of us by living good lives and doing good deeds. Yesterday is full of disappointment. Yesterday is full of stress and anxiety. Yesterday is filled with so many unfilled promises. Yesterday is full of anger and regret. Yesterday is over and there is nothing that can be done about yesterday to learn from the heartache of the past. When you learn tomorrow is filled with promise, tomorrow is filled with blessing if you have faith. Tomorrow is filled with great memories to be made with family and friends. Many of us speed through life not taking the time to enjoy the simple pleasures of the surrounding scenery. Some of us are so worried and stressed about tomorrow that it has taken our joy away. We can only live one day at a time so let's focus on doing that to the best of our ability of our lives. There is a lot of chaos all around us each and every day, you can have peace in the middle of chaos if you focus your mind and be thankful for life each and every day.

Time is of the essence. Make the best use of your time each and every day. If you are not careful you will look back on time and be like "where did it go?" and become regretful of the things you did not do. Treat people close to you with love and respect. Treat your lover with love and respect and date your lover. Keep the magic in your relationships fresh and alive. Appreciate what you have before it is too late. Show concern and help people when you get an opportunity. When you are playing cards and the dealer deals each player their hand, some of the players have a better hand than the other players. Still the player with the lesser hand can end up winning the game. How did the player with all the odds stacked against him win? The player with the odds stacked against him made wise decisions and played the hand he was dealt to the best of his ability. He did not give up or start complaining because he had a lesser hand. He kept battling until he won. This is the same in life just because you have been dealt an unfavorable hand does not mean you cannot win.

You can win if you have faith and become wise in your dealings. Life does not give everyone everything it wants we all have something you can use to our advantage. Enjoy life now. Don't wait until the perfect time; the time will never be perfect. There will always be something to deal with, some drama coming from some angle. Love your loved one's today because tomorrow is not promised. Many different things happen in the course of living life each and every day.

Take time to enjoy the moment. Even if things are not how you desire them to be in life at the moment, make it up in your mind to have joy. Stop crying over the stuff that happened yesterday. Don't even have bitterness in your heart. Forgive and let go. When you forgive you are really letting your heart heal. Slow down and enjoy the simple pleasures in life. We all have memories of good times and we have memories of bad times. We loved and cherish the good memories more in our heart. When you're driving sometimes, take the time to enjoy the simple pleasure of the surrounding scenery. Take time to enjoy your loved ones. No matter how your current situation is looking, you can make a comeback.

I was watching the Super bowl this past year. New England vs. Atlanta. The Patriots were trailing by 25 points midway through the third quarter. The Patriots never gave up, and they kept fighting. The Patriots fought back one play at a time; from Julian Edelman's miracle catch to the two point conversions. The Patriots never gave up and remained calm under pressure. The Patriots ended up coming back and winning the game because they kept fighting and never gave up. You can relate the Patriots victory to your life. You may be down today in life you can come back and win. Maybe you got fired or laid off from your job or some other situation. You may be down and wondering how you will get yourself back up. Much like the patriots if you get up each morning and be proactive in your life and never give up you can win.

You can get some lucky breaks along the way or blessings. Play by play from a sack to a lucky catch, the Patriots found themselves right back in the game after trailing behind. Day by day you can find yourself back in the game of life if you take steps to improve yourself and have a good mindset. In that same form, while the Atlanta Falcons were up big against the Patriots, they still lost because they lost focus of detail. You could be doing well today everything could change if you fail to remain humble. No matter how well things may seem to be going remain humble and always treat people with respect. Keep your caring attitude and don't become so nonchalant that you lose what helped to get where you are in the first place.

Chapter 11
Being an Overcomer

You can't control how people treat you or what they say to you can control your response. Don't let people easily anger you. People are dealing with many issues so just get back to your roots. If you don't have anything good to say don't say anything at all. Many times it is wise to just walk away and not engage in any confrontation. No matter what bad circumstance you encountered yesterday, you can reinvest yourself to succeed in life. Setbacks in life can be overcome and new goals and dreams can enter into your spirit. We are living in an age where we must put on strength and have hope that tomorrow will be better. We must overcome our anxiety and fear with a healthy balanced life of renewed focus and drive. Some days seem clear like a clear afternoon while others feel like thunder and lightning.

No matter how the day feels you must keep your focus and faith. Don't look at your life with sadness and remorse. Instead look at your life as an overcomer and someone who learned from setbacks. Even in the midst of tough situations, always keep your humor and optimism. Humor and optimism will help you see the light at the end of the tunnel and not to give up. We all face many different challenges and problems in life. Hardly anyone lives a problem free life, no matter how good you think you are. Some people handle their problems in different ways and different people have different coping strategies. Working out, helping people and volunteering are all-good coping strategies for dealing with stress. Failure is never fatal unless you give up trying. As long as you get up each morning you have a chance to turn failure into success. Be proactive with life and think of strategies you could employ to increase success.

Surviving in Between was written to look at where you currently are in life, giving inspiration to come up with strategies to improve your life and making the best out of tough situations. In life everyone will have some curveballs thrown their way and we must develop the confidence to move forward when facing an uncertain path. Tough times can build our character or they can make you feel fearful. Choose to have faith instead of becoming fearful. You can only drive your car for so long before you run out of gas. This is the same way in life. Living and running day to day you need a refill of faith from time to time. If you don't get your refill you will be running on empty, emotionally and everything else.

You know when you are not in a good emotional place because you will snap at people for the smallest stuff, even family and friends. When you feel yourself getting low emotionally, it is good to meditate and pray. It will also be good to be around good friends you trust or church members or people you can talk with. Try to stay away from gossip and pity parties. Pity parties kill you emotionally.

The thing that can help is coming up with solutions to resolve your issue. If you are going to be successful tomorrow, you cannot wallow in self-pity about what happened yesterday. Dry your tears and move on knowing that tomorrow is filled with promise if you don't give up. When life hands you a bad hand that turns your life on its head, you have the power to rebuild your life one day at a time. We can't control tomorrow we must have faith in the one who does. In the football game the team has to go 100 yards to score a touchdown. When the team trying to score they have opponents trying to stop them from scoring. Sometimes the teams trying to stop them get a sack, sometimes they get an interception, and sometimes the defense stops them and they get no yards. The team has to go to battle to get that 100 yards to score a touchdown. Many times in our lives we are sacked with many different problems. Sometimes we are sacked with worry, anxiety and fear. It looks as though life is whipping our asses and we don't know what to do to score or win.

Many times the problems in life have intercepted

our dreams and goals. On 1st down it looks like we are going nowhere. On 1st down we are having family problems and money problems. We get to 2nd down and we are having health problems and legal problems. We get to 3rd down and we are having mental problems. Our minds are so confused with issues we are facing that we don't know what to do. When we are facing 4th down, we can decide to punt or go for the 1st down. Sometimes in life you may have to punt and come up with different strategies to get the 1st down on tomorrow. You may have to come up with a different action plan or a different way of thinking to get the victory. On 4th down you can choose to go for it. You can choose not to be saddled by all your problems; you can choose to become an overcomer. You can choose to have faith to fight for that touchdown or first down. You can choose not to give up to fight for your family and meditate and pray through your problems.

No matter how the odds are not looking good in your favor, you can have a miracle catch along the way similar to the Patriots if you don't give up. You can be down today if you plant in your spirit you can come back day-by-day. Day by day if you action to win in life, you cannot only get back in the fame you could win and succeed. If one day doesn't go your way, just make it up in your mind that you will be back tomorrow. You will be back tomorrow with a good attitude you will be back tomorrow having learned the lessons of yesterday. You will be back tomorrow wiser and more determined than you were yesterday.

You can win if you don't quit and keep a good strong attitude no matter what is taking place in our lives or all around us. You can be surviving in between all kinds of different situations. Wake up and dress up knowing that you are beautiful, powerful and filled with potential. When you are having problems of all sorts, people speaking negative against you or you speaking or thinking negative thoughts against yourself, throw the negativity in the trash kick it out of your mind. You may ask me how does one kick it out of their mind? First watch what you allow to enter your spirit. Let the word of God enter your spirit. Listen to people who speak encouraging words and who talk about faith. Deal in the possibilities of the goodness of life.

Keep your head up and stay strong and encouraged. Many times the setbacks in your life propel you to new heights. When the war of life is raging, whether it is a health crisis or a legal crisis or some other crisis, you come to realize that you must enjoy the moments you live. Life teaches you many lessons. Lessons of being patient, faith, hope. You can develop a never to give up spirit if you don't quit. You can't change some of the tough situations you dealt with in the past. You can turn your obstacles and heartbreak of yesterday into ministry and helping people tomorrow. There have been a number of people who have turned their failure into successes. Michael Jordan was cut from his high school basketball team. Thomas Edison failed 37 times before inventing the light bulb. Babe Ruth struck out at bat 348 times. Many scientific laboratories use trial and error in accomplishing their goals.

Just because you have made some mistakes, learn from them and start over. A lot of our lives are filled with mistakes can be overcome with a good attitude and faith. In life we get busy sometimes with dealing with work stuff to the family situation. Even though you may be bust, always, take the time to take care of yourself mentally and emotionally. You can be so worried about other people that you yourself end up sick and mentally drained. If you are going to be strong for those around you, you must take care of yourself. Take 20 minutes out of the day each day to yourself to just unwind. Do things in your life that brings you joy. Whether its traveling or being around family and friends, getting your hair and toes done, going to church or your favorite sporting event, do things in your life that brings you joy. Volunteer for your favorite cause once a month or whenever your time permits. Do things that are meaningful to you.

We must choose to make the best of the gift of each

day we are blessed to see. Even if life currently is not all we expect or hope it will be, accept it as it is and always believe that better is coming. Live and laugh through the confusion, love through the pain, forgive even though you hurt and keep moving forward. The hands of time cannot be turned back, so we must not waste precious moments dwelling on regrets, failures, anger, grudges or anything negative. Purposely choose to focus on the good, the positive, the blessings of peace, joy, love, family and friends. We are in the time of day where we must cheat on our fears, take action, be proactive and get your joy back for living and serving others. We must break up with our doubts, the doubts that creep into our minds that hold us back, the doubts of low self-esteem, the doubts of nonbelief, the doubts of negativity in your mind.

We are in a time now where we must get engaged to our faith, have faith that everything is going to be alright, have faith you can have joy in the midst of any challenging circumstance around you, have faith that your family will be whole, have faith in whatever you hope for it can come to pass. We must become married to our goals and things we want to achieve. We must become married to our dreams. We must become married in the fact we can have peace in our minds and things around us. Many people blame the parents. You have people blaming this person or that person. At the end of the day, it is your life and you have to be responsible for all of it. Self-pity or a negative attitude will get you nowhere in life.

Many people have overcome great challenges to be successful. Have you ever been somewhere and then something told you to leave? After you left you get home and hear about the shooting that took place and you just had left. Always learn to listen to your intuition or your instincts. You don't need someone preaching to you; you know deep down inside when something is not right. Listening to your instincts can keep you away from dangers. From time to time, we all have to deal with crazy situations and sometimes we even have to deal with crazy acting people. If we are not careful, that craziness will affect our mental stability and end up having us feel as if we are crazy. Although we are not able to control what comes before us, we are able to control what we allow our minds to meditate on. Meditate on the word and on good thoughts. Pray over situations that are bothering you.

If you happen to fail in life, don't get depressed and all bent out of shape. Fight your way back up and start with new aspirations and goals. In life you must be willing to take risks in your career, love, or any other goal you must have set for yourself. There are no guarantees in life, you must be willing to take some risks so you will not live with regrets. In the football game when the team is trying to score, the defense comes up with different plots and schemes to avoid the offense from getting a first down or scoring a touchdown. In our lives there are plots and schemes that the enemy has devised for our downfall. So as the offense is trying to go 100 yards to get a touchdown there are some plots that the defense has to come up with to stop them. As you are living life day-to-day everything will not always be easy. Same as with the offense trying to score, there will be challenges and difficult moments.

When you are living your life, there will be challenging and difficult moments. If we have faith we can get through those challenging and difficult moments, not only can we get through those challenging and difficult moments also we can get stronger during our hardships. We get closer to the Lord during our hardships and we learn of him on a different level. You must put it in your spirit deep down in your soul we must develop the tenacity to face and embrace life's many challenges and hardships. If you don't have the fight tenacity in your spirit, you will be beaten by life's unpredictable challenges. We must have the courage to stand up and face the many different crises' life will throw our way. We must feel the fear and do it anyway.

A great thing about the word of God it helps you develop the mental strength when facing challenges from all kinds of different directions. When something bad happens to you, you can choose to go into depression and cry about it all day and night, or you can choose to have faith and live. Choosing to have faith that no matter what comes along you will live and survive. If you choose to develop your faith, you can withstand many different challenges you will have to encounter.

It is important to be positive and optimistic because miracles can happen when you are positive. If you have been through tough situations in your life, tell it to other people who are feeling hopeless. Tell people how your hardships made you a better person. There are a lot of people hopeless out here and each one of us can be a teacher. Some people are reading this book and grieving over the loss of a loved one. Years later it still hurts the best thing you can do in the grieving process is letting it go. Some days will be easier than others when you are grieving you owe it to yourself and your family to let it go. There are no benefits to holding onto grief, anger and situations that happened yesterday. There is nothing that can be done about yesterday and when you let it go you are available to help other family members. As you rise to face each new day, leave that spirit of heaviness and despair that's been trying to weigh you down. Dispose in the trash the worries, the fears, the anxieties and the doubts. Overwhelming odds may be stacked against you you can overcome anything with the right mindset and faith. No matter what's going on in your life always keep your sense of humor and laugh. Laughter is healing for the soul.

Keeping your wits about you when facing tough circumstances will help you remain positive when surrounded by negative forces. You can choose to live your life in denial or depression. Or, you can keep choosing to walk through life knowing that the circumstances you are currently in is serving a higher purpose. Some of us grew up in ghettos. We saw people get killed. We grew up with our parents on drugs and alcohol. We grew up some night's hungry not knowing what we would eat. Some of us had our parents get killed, loved one's die in car wrecks or from health problems. Some of us have been through some tough situations. What those tough situations teach you is to persevere during the pain. Hold your head up during the rough times. Taking things one day at a time and being the best you can be each day will help you overcome pain. When African Americans were slaves working in the fields, going through all kinds of horror, they did not know that one day we would be gifted with a black president. They had faith when they were out on the fields and suffering horror that their seeds would overcome. All of what our ancestors did for us; we should be inspired to live a life to make them proud and to keep walking through our adversity.

When you feel fear hovering around your life, visualize all you ancestors walking beside you as you take your steps forward. Pace yourself and your emotions. Don't let yourself swing from going way up to way down. Control your emotions with meditation or doing some things you enjoy doing. Don't let your emotions control you. When things happen in your life and you can't explain it, be optimistic that everything will work out fine.

You can stay up all night worrying about different issues. Have faith and be optimistic that you are an overcomer and be confident the winds will calm down. Many of us face great opposition are great anyways. Don't just sit on the sidelines of life when people have died for you to take center stage. Give your gift to the world, we all don't have everything, we all have something Doubts never achieved anything, only action and faith achieved and added value to your life and those around you. Wake up each morning and tell yourself "I can do this". There are many pages in the book of life. One page or even one chapter may not be good. Keep on living, keep on turning the page and soon your story will be great. If one day is not good, learn from that day and come back better the next day. In life you can go through times where you lose your job, homes, businesses and in some cases your freedom. When crisis and chaos hit your life, you can use it to help you grow and make you better, or you can cave and become a failure.

There is no situation, no matter how bleak it looks, that cannot be turned around. Times of shaking and uncertainty will come. Life's events will be tossed around and everything we thought we could count on seems to no longer be dependable. The shaking in our lives can bring about some good. When life seems to be coming apart at the core, we must tune into the word of the Lord, focus and have faith. We will not understand everything that happens to us, some things are divinely ordered to help us to be more focused and to gain more faith. Sometimes we could be on the wrong path and something goes wrong to get us to changes paths.

There is no need to feel sorry for yourself about the things that happened yesterday. Get back into the game of life, dust off your shoulders, dry your tears and begin each new day with vigor and hope. Life can be messy and unpredictable at times. It forces us to re-examine our relationships and goals for the future. We can shape our attitudes in a good way when life's unpredictable moments hit us. Choose to speak good words to yourself and others. Words can build you up or tear you down. Choose your words carefully to build yourself up and those around you. You can look at a job loss as an opportunity to get a better job. You can look at any failure you are faced with on the positive side. There are lots of different circumstances that we are faced with, how we respond can make a huge difference. You may be reading this book and you find you are in transition. You may be looking for a job or a career, you may find yourself getting a divorce, or even thinking about moving to a different city.

Life can make you feel lost at times, the world is full of people who overcome challenges each and every day. You are never the lone danger, no matter what situations you face. It's good to have food friends you can talk to about your problems, even if you don't have friends, meditation is a good outlet to let your problems out. If you are not satisfied with your life, come up with a list of action plans you can take each day to improve your life. Don't just skip out on that networking event, go and show up. There is power in meeting and shaking hands. Do things that bring you joy each day and do things that will help you become successful.

Take the initiative to make your relationships better. The way you speak with people, your tone of voice could make a big difference. Sometimes you can get into a habit of going to work, going home or maybe to the gym. The freshness has left your life. Do things that make the freshness come back alive in your life. Listen to your heart and listen to your gut.

When you are making decisions, you need clarity on the direction to go. When you get to the point where life has become overwhelming and you don't know which way to turn, sometimes you may need some rest. So take the day off, catch up on your sleep and refocus your mind on what has to get done. Some days we need to recharge our minds, bodies and soul. Everyday won't be perfect that does not mean it won't have purpose. Go out and be active in your local community, help out your favorite causes.

When you just isolate yourself in the house, your problems can begin to seem more than what they are. You must get up each day with hope in your heart that things will become better. You must find hope even if you are behind prison bars or even the slums of the ghetto. Always wake up something each day to be hopeful for. You may be reading this book and thinking things are so bleak in my life. Everywhere I turn around and look there are problems. Hope will sustain you even when you are facing some tough situations. Many people commit suicide each year because they lose hope. Hope will help you become proactive in accomplishing goals and never giving up. All of us have faced some dark moments in our lives and when we face those dark moments, we must take corrective action to make the days brighter.

No matter how bleak situations may seem you can find things in your life to be grateful for. Focus on the positive and the things that are going right in your life instead of focusing on what is wrong. Focus on the people who are there for you when things are not going well. There are people in the hospital beds with life threatening illness, given only a few years to live. Some of the people in the hospital overcome the odds because they have the right attitude. They refuse to give into complaining and negative attitudes. What is one action you could take to improve your circumstance? Keep your sense of humor in the confusing dark moments in life. Laugh through the pain of life, dance through the confusion, and sing through the heartache. Challenges in life will come; there is no way to avoid them.

Instead of seeing them as stumbling blocks or wondering "why me?" we can change our perspective and see them as stepping stones and trust that the good Lord will strengthen us with the power to overcome each and every day. The challenges of life can grow your faith. Stay away from negative people, they can kill your spirit. Negative people suck away your enthusiasm for life, hurt your confidence and can impair your vision. Be in tune with your spirit and your goals you want to achieve. Block out the naysayers and the people who plant doubts in your soul.

In life our paths will be different and we will all face

our fair share of disappointment, heartache and pain, we will have to encounter doubts fears and naysayers. All hell will break loose from time to time and you must find the inner strength to pull through. Many times it breaks our hearts to see our teenage kids acting like they have no sense. We have seen the struggle and want our kids to avoid the pitfalls in life. Many times we have to sit back and let our kids fall for them to realize what we was telling them the whole time. We pray for our kids, at the end of the day we can hope that life lessons will teach them and they change before it's too late. When living life day-to-day, it is the people that are closest to us that hurt us the most sometimes. They can just inject us with their fears, doubts and negativity. We can love them, when they come with their doubts and negativities, we must tune them out or on our deaf ear stay devoted to our goals and dreams.

You will face nonbelievers in your daily living. During times of chaos in your life it is important to stay away from people who constantly add to the stress of your life. Some people you encounter always will whine and complain. Some people have no joy because they're always blaming someone else for their problems and situations. During times of transition we need to have a focused mind and a determined spirit. People who constantly add to the stress of your life are not good for your health. When your mind is not on track it is good to be around people who pick you up. When you are facing conflict, it is good to be in tune with the word of the Lord. If the thoughts are not encouraging, you need to put a deaf ear on to it. People are dealing with their own issues in their life; it is important to not let their negative aspects of life inject into your spirit. Focus on keeping the spirit of positivity around you and continue to be helpful in the areas where you can.

Life forces you to love people from a distance. One of the reasons I wrote this book was to inspire hope and encourage reading because it is good for the soul. You know this is a testimony and your test this is a ministry for your pain. There is hope for the times you have felt hopeless, there is wisdom in the times you've failed. We all make mistakes and when we start getting older we wonder where to go. You may not be that far from where the Lord intended you to be. He can still make a whole lot of you never lose your hope for a better tomorrow or for your happiness. We must never lose hope in our kids.

If you have a goal, seek out people or volunteer opportunities that will assist you accomplishing your goals. No matter your age, where you come from or your background, you can overcome any of the odds placed in your path. You can't look for other people to rescue you from your problems; you can look to the person in the mirror. Each day you wake up in the morning start speaking positivity over your life. Many times we let the negative self-talk get the best of us. We whisper stuff in our spirit, such as, "I can't do this, life is so messed up and many other negative things. Replace those negative thoughts with thoughts of hope. For example, I can do this, life is getting better, and I would be a good husband, father or friend. Don't be your own worst critic; develop a habit of speaking faith. No matter what happened yesterday, get over it and take responsibility for your future.

To my brothers out there, don't become upset when people tell you need to get a job. If you have kids and a family, you should want to help take care of them. Yes! We all fall down, don't stay down. You can make your job going out looking for a job. When you take one step, the Lord will take one with you. Don't just sit around all day complaining and doing nothing. You can do something! Slow money is better than no money. Even if you only make nine dollars per hour, the Lord said if you be faithful over small, he will make you ruler over much (Matthew 25:23).

Have faith! Nobody owes it to you to take care of you; you owe it to yourself to take care of yourself. Take steps every day to improve, to look for a job (if you are unemployed), go to networking events and meetings. Sometimes when I ride, I see a prostitute walking down the street. When I see this woman strung out on drugs, I think about my daughters. I think to myself, "She could have been a doctor, lawyer, school teacher, dentist or something more productive. One reason we are so disappointed in our kids is because we see the potential they have, sometimes we feel they're just wasting their life. One thing about hope is that it is never too late to change.

Chapter 12
Life is about choices

You can begin again, whether you're reading this book from prison, or a mansion. No matter what your luck has been in life, you may have been told by the world that you will not amount to anything, you may be strung out on drugs and can't stop drinking, you could be homeless or living as a prostitute to support your drug habit, no matter what situation you find yourself in you can overcome and become an inspiration. You may have been crippled yesterday by the hardships of the past, you can walk again when you have faith and you are determined. When you have faith, the good Lord will make your life worth living, you can dramatically change your life. Life is full of people who have overcome tremendous odds and became successful. It is vital that to make conscious and constant daily actions to improve your life. You must save your own life before you can help the surrounding people; vision yourself overcoming and getting out of that bad situation. Your life may be filled with insurmountable odds, if you keep that hope and determination in your spirit, you can overcome.

Take responsibility for your actions, develop resilience and even when circumstances want to make you give up, imagine your enemies laughing. Live to spite the enemy and to be an inspiration to someone who is on the verge of giving up. Sometimes, life can make you bitter and you just want to cry. It's okay to be bitter and cry for a night. When the crying is over, dump the bitterness from your heart and start your day refreshed and re-evolved in forgiveness. Bitterness does your soul and spirit no good. When you forgive, you help your soul to begin again. When life seems too dark, we must cling to the hope that things will change. Sometimes negative things in life happen for a reason, we will never understand suffering though.

Bad things can cause some good to happen to us and we won't realize it. You can gain wisdom through trial, error and suffering. Many things happen in our life and we are like, "Why me?" Just take on the attitude that when adverse events hit your life, you will take the good from it and grow. You can put yesterday behind you. Take it as a lesson learned and reinvest your future. Staying positive and humble will help you bounce back and overcome these circumstances. The people that bounce back in life, develop a faith come hell or high water, they will fight for the life they want. Stop blaming others for your setbacks in life and start working on building a better life for yourself. Develop a resilient spirit and get around good people that will speak life into a debt situation.

It is always a good to take good advice from people who have been through similar things. Or, good people whom you trust. That's why it is good for some young married couples to have friendships with older married couples and try to ask for their advice on certain situations. The older married couples have wisdom because sometimes they have been faced similar situations and overcame it. Also, It's is good for kids to listen to their parents and teachers on certain things because many times the parents are caring adults who has faced similar situations. Always have goals and be productive with your life, even when it seems it's not going anywhere. Keep that hope for a better tomorrow alive in your spirit. Choose to be positive, have faith, to cast down the negative self-talk and to be on the positive side of life. Always choose hope over hopeless, faith over doubt, positive attitude over a negative one and respect over disrespect.

No matter which choices we made yesterday, play in your spirit to become wise in choices. Great things happen when you are optimistic and determined. Hold on to your dreams as a child would, for the time will come and you will be into adulthood and your dreams can come to pass. Stay away from dreams killers and people that want to get you into drugs, gangs and things you know you have no business being a part of. There is a better way. We must also be aware of what enters our spirit through music. Don't let the sad music of today's music be the music of your life, develop a new tone of music; the tone of hopefulness, overcoming, encouragement and surviving and thriving. A new song of hope is what we need. If you are not careful, some of the music you listen to will have you feeling down. No matter your age, keep your magic of living alive in your spirit. Life will not be easy; some days will be better than others. Keep your determination and as your living one day at a time, it will become better. Nothing is built in one day, it takes many days of planning to build. So each day, be proactive, take charge of your life and deal each and every day. We all have different dreams and goals that we would like to accomplish. When you keep striving and thriving for a better tomorrow, then a better tomorrow will find you.

It's my goal with writing this book that it will inspire you to overcome and achieve your dreams. Become the author of your own life. Wake up each day with purpose; come up with some goals that will support your purpose. Regain your passion for living and achieving. Always have the same passion for your family and community just as you have passion for your favorite sports teams. Imagine the possibilities you can achieve if you keep a good attitude coupled with determination and faith. You have the power to change your tomorrow, to determine if you will become positive or negative, and to be anything you set your mind out to be. We owe it to the people who came before us, those who fought and suffered tremendously, our ancestors. Going forward, let's take steps to improve our lives and better our communities.

Whatever path you're on, just realize nothing happens overnight and you may encounter some tough days and nights. Sometimes life will not go as planned, so be open to the adventures. Many people get a college degree in one field and end up doing something totally different in another field. Keep your values about yourself; become a person of your word, have integrity and use the values that your grandparents or parents taught you. You know when something isn't right, let your instinct guide you. Don't become a lover of money.

Many people make mistakes in life because of their love for money. When I was an insurance agent, I learned to always have morals and integrity in my dealings. No matter what mistakes you made yesterday, learn from and grow from it and use it to make you a better person. When things get rough in your life, gain some encouragement on the things in the past you have overcome. Be proud of your past and some hardships you conquered. Let your past encourage you. Think about when you were in a bad situation and how the Lord helped you to overcome. There has been some of you that could have been killed, the Lord kept you here.

Think about some accomplishments you wanted to achieve and accomplish them. In the face of the odds, let your past inspire you to forge ahead in renewed focus and determination. Some of us was raised in the hood, we still overcame and got our degrees and made something of our lives. Others are simply striving and thriving in our lives. Always seek out from different walks of life and gaining wisdom. Whatever you want to accomplish, seek out the people who are already are accomplished in the area. If you cannot find those people, seek to do volunteer work in that area to gain the knowledge and the wisdom needed.

To the game makers around the world, especially if you are older, you should make it your duty to help out the younger guys and tell them the dangers of committing crime and how it will ruin their life and devastate the community.

Moreover, I was raised in the ghetto and my mother made a living selling her body while my father was an alcoholic. Well, how many times did you hear the Gospel preached? How many times did you hear something to tell you that there is a God that loves you? People always want to blame society, their parents, again you must take responsibility for your own actions. Surviving and in between is a book written to help you see things in a different light and inspire hope in your heart. Over generations your experiences and knowledge is valuable in the uplifting and encouraging the younger generation. When you help, volunteer, or give that word of advice it gives you a connection to the community and future generation will thank you. When I was in high school at Austin East High School in Knoxville, TN, there was a teacher named Mrs. Seely that always spoke life into me. Even though growing up in the hood was hard some days, she always encouraged me to stay on the right path and don't get involved in drugs and crime. Her hopes, coupled with some hard truths, helped me down the road once I got older. A lot of times kids don't didn't realize and appreciate the good advice parent's give. Years down the road to adulthood, they will hang on to those words in their memory.

You may have lost your job, or a loved one could have died. Right now is bleak and you may feel lost. When you are dealing with chaos in your life, it would be great to be around some uplifting people. They have all different types of organizations and support groups. You can do a Google search and many times larger churches have different support groups where you can share your concerns fears or just have someone to talk to. You are never alone in what you are going through; there are many people going through what you are going through and much more. Situations in our lives will require us to make some transitions. Whether it is a divorce a loss of a job death of a loved one or something else.

Sometimes you have to transition in order to remain optimistic and determine what will help during your transition in life. You can find yourself ministering to other people, you need someone to minister to you. You could be pouring out in other people's lives. At times you need someone to pour into yours. You can't be making sure everyone in the family is good, are you aren't making sure yourself is good. Be sure to do those things to make you are all right emotionally, mentally and spiritually. The wisdom of a support group or the wisdom of people that went before you are like a life jacket when you are drowning in your problems. Life does not seem as bad when you have someone to talk to and share lessons of wisdom with. You learn wisdom through observing other people's lives, as well as yours. Life experiences rules are made for your good, so you will not get into a crash or dangerous situation. It's dangerous for kids to ignore their parent's warnings.

Don't lose your mind when you are faced with adverse situations. You should seek help and your faith, control your emotions and don't let your emotions control you. Maintain a healthy look on life no matter what situation you find yourself in. What can keep you going in life is thinking about your children and family. Knowing that your community needs help and having the opportunity to serve should make the minutes of your days count. It is not good when you have a family and are doing nothing to support them. At least try to get a job on a daily basis, or try to do volunteer events each month. If you just sit around all day idling away your time when you could be doing something productive, is sad. Some of my brothers have given up on life, I challenge you after reading this book, to think of a way you can get back into the game of life. If you are reading this from prison, there are church activities and different programs you can involve yourself in. Make yourself productive and when you come home, leave the life of crime and start fresh.

Be a person of integrity, honesty, of your word, be responsible for yourself and never assume someone else will take care of you. People are funny; one minute they love you, the next minute they hate you. Always be a person of respects and if people help you that is fine. Always depend on yourself. Make doing the right things part of your D.N.A. whether people are watching, or not. No situations you encounter are permanent and having the right attitude and spirit is important. Life will teach you valuable lessons and you will gain courage, or run in fear. Having friends or people to talk to when times get rough can help you greatly.

We all share common life experiences. Many of us face different challenges at different chapters in our lives. As Surviving in Between comes to a close, I want to encourage you that your life experiences will make you wiser in life or humble you. Every day that you wake up is a gift from the Lord. Miracles happen every single day to those who refuse to give up and keep their sense of humor during the chaos of life. There are some people who the doctors have given six months to live. Instead of caving into depression, they develop a faith and renowned Spirit. They go on to live many years past six months because they developed the right mindset. My father, Lawrence "Butch" William Senior, developed cancer, and it was looking bad for him. He started researching his diagnosis and stopped using drugs and alcohol. He even started workout for an hour each day. My father is still with us and he continues to fight each day. When you have the right mindset, you can overcome challenges. Your family might not be the traditional one and things may be rough, you still can have joy under any circumstance.

Ask the good Lord for guidance in contemplating your next career and for the things you want in the future. Life sometimes can be nonstop action, so we always must look to make improvements in the areas where we are not strong. Apply these strategies in your everyday life to develop a strong mindset, we can't always control what happens in our lives, we can have a good attitude and stay positive.

I hope that you are enjoying this book so much that you order it again and share it with your friends on Facebook and Instagram.

Love your community and your family, not just by words, in your actions as well. Love your community by mentoring some lost teenagers or gangbangers. Love your family by being proactive in providing and watching the words that you speak. Remember to always speak in a tone of love. Love has little to do with actions in your (HERE) deeds life is short. Create memories with your loved ones before it's too late. Be kind to everyone you meet you never know what battles they are facing in a world full of noise everywhere you go. Sometimes in your car or your home, let the quietness rule your world. It allows you to think clearly, it also is a chance to sit in tune with your spirit. Become constant with whatever life throws your way and find happiness. Always want to improve, make sure you find some joy, even in the mindset of mess.

Growing up in Walter P. Taylor Homes with my dad, my sister Patrice and my brother Lawrence, who was older many and at times he said with grandma. Growing up in the projects, one thing we had was happiness. We didn't have a lot, but our community loved each other. So, if I did something crazy, the community would get on me before I even got home. We could sleep with the doors open and I didn't have to worry about someone breaking in. we didn't have a lot, we did have happiness in our community. I know some people reading this book can also attest that they didn't have a lot, had love and happiness. Each and every day you achieve something, celebrate it. If you've been clean from drugs and alcohol for one month celebrate. Celebrate your milestone, the big ones and the small ones.

Slow down in the rush of life and spend time with the important people in your life. You can become so busy that you miss out. Don't rush the beautiful moments in life, live in the moment and appreciate the joy of each positive experience. Life will force you to move on after a death of a loved one. Life can be devastating if you allow it. Our loved one's want us to move on and be happy. When someone dies that you love, they will forever be tied to you in your heart. You are responsible for your own happiness and are the captain of your soul. You create the songs in your life. Let your life be inspired by the people who came before you. Every day you talk to some people that live in the regret of yesterday; where they talk about who they used to be yesterday. Ladies, don't even bring up the bad memories with your man from yesterday; forgive and move on. Some women always bring up stuff from the past and it doesn't do anyone any good. Whether it is lovers or friends get over the best situation from yesterday because when you do you are freeing your mind body and spirit.

Just as the person who goes to the gym each day to work out their body to be in good shape, your have to do the same to your mind; feeding it good thoughts and uplifting, encouraging words. Do what you know in your heart is the right thing to do, don't worry about what people may think, they are not living your life for you. There's so much to deal with in life; so much conflict and stress. It's important to try to identify some of the stressors in your life and dump them in the trashcan of your memory. Practice being good and doing the right things all the time. Even when you can do wrong, you don't want to be faced with karma because when you do stuff you know in your heart karma will pay you a visit. Some things we do and bad stuff happens out the blue and you wonder where it came from, You must take inventory on how you are conducting your life, it pays to do the right thing and to treat people with respect and kindness.

When I get in my car I ride around different hoods in America. There are so many brothers just hanging around wasting their time. I think it would be good for the brothers to learn how to do plumbing, electrical and mechanical work; stuff that will help them becomes self-sufficient. If you are reading this and your life seems to be going nowhere, think of some steps that you could take to improve your situation.

Life will test you. Lawyers, and doctors and many other professionals had to be tested various times to make sure they were qualified to do the job. In your life you will encounter many tests to make sure you are real. Be positive when you are facing the tests knowing that you have everything in you you need to past. Sometimes during the test of life you fail because we cursed someone out that was rude to us. Now those times when we fail, we can learn from the failure and take a different approach on the test and pass. Always recognize that the preachers, leaders and people who are always trying to encourage. The people that are perceived to be the strongest among us are the one's who smile through silent pain, secretly cry behind closed doors. They also fight battles no one knows about. It can be the people you come in contact with every day that need an encouraging words. Life requires both urgency and patience. People can ruin good things if they lack the patients needed.

We need patience with our loved ones, our jobs

and many other situations. Where counsel on a daily basis you have to be urgent about making efforts to improve circumstances in life. Patience is required about seeing the fulfillment of many of our goals. Greatness can come out of pain hardship, chaos and despair. Many of today's greatness people that you see on T.V. and read about came from tough times. Tough times don't last forever, people do. Develop toughness about yourself that you put way down in your D.N.A. You know that space between a rock and a hard place? That's where greatness happens. Remember in life that what goes in to your spirit, must come out. If you are only putting negativity in your spirit, then that's what will come out. If that's the only thing you're feeding your spirit, it's no wonder you cuss out the waitress at the restaurant when she makes a mistake. It's no wonder that you wake up depressed or with a bad attitude, because your spirit is filled with junk.

If you are filling your mind and spirit with positivity, like listening to gospel or uplifting music. Then when the waiter messes up on your order, you don't curse them out. Instead, you have patience and understanding. When your spirit is right, your whole frame of mind begins to change. Separate yourself from negativity and watch how your thoughts process, even your vocabulary will change and improve. Negativity can come in many forms: people, music, thoughts and many other forms. When you feel it coming, cast it out. If you fall down, don't stay down. Make your way back up with strategic steps.

The comeback is the most important part. Let the pain of yesterday fuel your fire in your bones for the success of tomorrow. After you get done reading this book become inspired, there are some close associates around you that counted you out. Prove to them, survive and thrive. Prove them wrong and the fact that they could not count. Hardships often prepare ordinary people for greatness. Count your blessings in life, there are many people who wish they could be in your shoes. There are people that are going through what you are going through, and worse. Be kind to people you encounter on a daily basis your word and your smile may be the only thing that they need to hear and see to turn their whole life around. Let go of what you can't control; we can't control yesterday or some things that's happened in the past. Let forgiveness rule your spirit and get over anything that causes you to be bitter about yesterday.

Listen to your heart and spirit on what directions and actions to take. Take a deep breath, live and be active. Let calmness roll over your day. Let productivity each day rules your life. When you make goals and are productive each and every day the things you will be hoping for will meet you in common hours. Life will take you through some painful experiences and humble your soul. Some thing's happened in our lives that we don't understand. Some stuff hit us out the blue and we must have faith that we will get through it. Sometimes we are disappointed in ourselves for putting ourselves in the situation to be arrested. We can look back over our lives and we are disappointed by some situations we allowed ourselves to get into. There are some steps we could have taken or some things we could have done differently to avoid the situation.

Life has many turns and sped bumps. Some things we don't see coming, no matter what comes our way we must let faith grow. When you were going through your dark days, it is important not to withdraw from life. Go out to meet and talk to people, this will help your mood. Do things you enjoy doing, go out and exercise. Surviving in between is a book written to support and challenge your way of thinking. As we grow older and hence wiser, we slowly realize that wearing a $300 or a $30 watch, they both tell the same time. Whether we carry a $500 or a $50 handbag, the amount of money inside is the same. Whether the house we live in is 300 or 3,000 Sq Ft. Lonely is the same whether you drive $8,000 Honda or $80,000 Benz, they both serve the same purpose. You will realize your true happiness does not come from the material things of the world. When you have true friendship, people who you laugh and kick it with all day and all night about old memories, that is true happiness. People that love you will love you because when there are a million reasons to give up the people that love you will find one reason to hold on.

Chapter 13
Skip over the Pain and Survive

The six best doctors in the world are:
Sunlight- there has been many studies done that show that sunlight makes you feel better. Rest- you have to rest your body to recharge. Many times you need to recharge mentally and emotionally. Exercise- many doctors will tell patients that they need to exercise to improve their health. Diet-you cannot eat everything that looks good. Some foods that you are eating are the reasons for have blood pressure and many other illnesses. Get into the habit of eating better. Self-confidence and friends- having good friends is a blessing to have. Good friends are like sunshine and on a rainy day. The older we get the more we enjoy the simple pleasures of life, such as peace of mind. It is my hope that this book sells and does well. If it can help at least one person, then the book has had an impact. What does not kill you makes you stronger and better. There is an old saying, "storms make trees take deeper roots. As I started writing this book, I research the saying to get a better understanding of its meaning. After a heavy rainfall

water gets into the ground, on a deeper level. The trees water-seeking roots follow the water and implant themselves down deeper.

Many people that study trees also believe that the stress of storm winds causes the outer layers of a tree's trunk to grow faster, helping it to thicken up in a short period of time. It's not just one storm though that helps the tree grow deeper and stronger where it stands, it's s several storms over time, a series of torrents and gusts. All of the rooting and growing in the face of heavy weather. It protects the tree from simply blowing over and it prepares a tree for the storms that are yet to come. Just because a tree remains standing, does not mean it's not damaged. When lightning strikes it almost always leaves scars. A tree may be alive and well-a survivor-yet bear marks that never fully fade. It if some injuries never heal, do scars speak to survival, or death. Perhaps both, if we think of scars as small parts that died in order to save the whole.

People who have been through circumstances can relate to this tree concept. Some trouble can damage you so deeply that even though you are here physically, your mind has not fully recovered. So, It's hard to be mentally present after such horrible times. Some trouble you go through and wonder if your mind, body and soul will ever be the same. Some storms will pass quickly while others take years and it takes a toll on your spirit. Often, we aren't even aware of a storms full impact until after the fact, when we have the visibility to sort out all the damage. These last few years have been a challenging time for a few of us. You can be waiting for some good things to happen, then out of nowhere trouble hits. When the trouble hits, you are sometimes dealing with months of stress and worry. People always say to keep our spirits up and things will get better.

However, when you're going through it, it doesn't seem like you're every getting any relief. Some mornings you may wake up thinking, "Can we just fast forward and skip over the pain and heartache?" There is a saying, "If you want the rainbow, you have to put up with the rain." Rainbows appear in the sky, but only after the clouds have cleared. So, you can look forward to the rainbow after every storm. If by chance you cannot see a rainbow after your storm, you should simply look and hope for one.

The rainbow is a symbol of promise; a beautiful reminder of the beauty after a storm has passed. Tit is also a symbol of hope for a brighter future for tomorrow. As we live each day and wake up every morning, many of us are celebrating graduations, good jobs, good health and other great accomplishments at work and in love. But, it's important that we also reflect on the suffering, sacrifice and scars of yesterday.

After the storm is over, rise and be filled with a new hope and promise. Some storms in your life can make you better if you keep the right perspective. You can live a productive life and become happier if you take actual steps to achieve. A newborn baby just don't wake up and start way walking overnight right out of the mothers womb. The baby started out crawling, then taking baby steps. Day-by-day the baby will get better at walking and eventually starting running around everywhere. Maybe you're not living as productive as you want to live right now. Maybe you are not satisfied with the way things are in your life right now. But, If you start like the baby did by crawling, and then you can go on to taking baby steps. Eventually, you will find your happiness. When you start out crawling, you can do this by being thankful for each and every day. Become thankful over the little things in your life. Once you become thankful, day-by-day you will find yourself getting stronger and becoming happier in life. There will be times when people will say to us, "The test will come in your response." So, choose to watch over your words and actions when confronted with conflict. When you choose to take the high road, instead of cursing them out, then you know that you are growing day-by-day.

A real friend will not always tell you positive things,

they will be encouraging while you transition to better things. Sometimes the truth is not always good and positive is that it will be encouraging and mixed with reality and faith. Some of the obstacles and challenges we have to face are not fair. Those obstacles and challenges that you face creates a better you in the long run and your faith is developed on a whole other level of the furnace of convict. This book has given you an example of how the storms can make you better if you keep the right mindset. When I watch some people paint or draw it amazes how good some artists are. They can paint whatever they see without missing a beat. When they get going on the outline, initially you would think it would be a good painting once they finish it is awesome. When you are faced with that trouble, initially you don't know this will benefit you when you make it through the trip you learn some valuable lessons. Sometimes trouble comes to humble us and it helps develop us. As good people develop a high opinion of yourself take care of yourself and your body. Stop being down on yourself about something that happened yesterday. Forgive yourself and forgive other people who have wronged you in some sort.

When you forgive him let go of the grudges. You are giving yourself the chance to have peace. When you forgive, you open yourself up for good things to happen in your life. Forgiveness is good for your health and bitterness is bad for your health. Google bitterness and cancer when you get time. We all have things in our life that we wish was different. We all wish our mother was Oprah Winfrey and our father was Michael Jordan and we don't want to be born in the ghetto. We do not want our mothers on drugs and alcohol and do not want our fathers on drugs and alcohol either. We want the perfect family and to be raised in the perfect situation. Many times in our lives we were raised under tough circumstances, those tough circumstances can motivate us to want to do better. Those tough circumstances that you grew up in could develop your tenacity to succeed. Some of the kids that have rich parents wish they had your peace of mind. You have some people that are only rich in money. Choose to be happy no matter where you find yourself at in life. If you are a worker at a job then it is your desire to move up in a higher position. Work harder in your current place and be happy until your number's called. Buildings are not built overnight. Don't get into a restaurant to be a wonder overnight. We cannot get into things to rush things. You can get yourself in a mass trying to rush the process. It's OK to want more all things take the proper timing. The grass isn't greener on the other side; the grass is greener where you water your yard. Water your yard with a good attitude, hope and contentment.

Some women meet the guy and he broke, he tries plus he treats you with respect. He has a vision for the future the woman is unhappy because he can't afford to buy her things she wants right now. The woman is looking at her friends and what they have, so she stops supporting her man because she's so focused on what her friends got that she is taking her man for granted. The best relationship starts when you're struggling together and you grow together. You can apply this situation to a number of different scenarios in your life, the important part to remember is to be happy where you are. It may not be where you want to be, take steps each day to be where you want to be. Some of the couples who have been married twenty or thirty years, one thing they always tell me is that they have become two forgivers. The current situation that we found ourselves in can mature us in ways we never imagined. There is a purpose for your pain. If you are not happy when you are broke and living in the tiny apartment you would not be happy when you start being able to live in the big house. Don't miss the beautiful memories of today by thinking about the problems of tomorrow. Become thankful for what you have. There are millions of people wishing they were in your shoe.

As you are reading this book, I am not sure what season of life you were in be thankful and become comfortable in the skin that you are in. You don't have to be boastful, let confidence rule inside your soul. Live your life. You don't have to compare your life to anyone else to be the best you can be. Hold in your goals and don't let weak-minded people make you feel intimidated. In life, all of us have different coping strategies. When you are faced with different circumstances that we encounter even with your kids, if you have more than one, some of your kids can take more and maybe the other kids you try different strategies because maybe they may be sensitive. Some kids you can look at and they will straighten up and other kids you may have to jack them up. In your dealings in your life, aim to be a good person no matter what. Celebrate yourself and the obstacles you have overcome. You maybe celebrating that you used to have a bad attitude or used to go off on people. Now you have become more patient and you watch the words you use when dealing with people.

There are many situations you could have overcome. Celebrate those accomplishments and aim for better. When you are facing a tough time it is easy to become negative and speak things we should not. Take on a new attitude when trouble invades your space. Take on an attitude that this will not destroy me, my joy will come back. Everything is in your perspective. Whatever occupies your mind will control which way your life is moving. Occupy your thoughts with action plans, succeeding, prospering and improving. If you plan on things getting better in your mind, self-doubt can no longer stay there. Visualize you live in the good home. Visualize your business succeeding and visualize good health in relationships. Visualize yourself laughing with good memories of the struggles of yesterday. Make a vow to yourself today you will be more intentional in focus with your time. Be disciplined in your pursuits and stay motivated. Even when things get hard, keep your sense of humor about you and smile during the chaos. Don't be like the people who are just living indifferent, just drinking and smoking their time away. So many people are not doing anything productive. They don't work or volunteer; they don't try to better themselves in any form or fashion. Seems like they are just wasting their time, giving no effort.

Fight for your happiness; develop your passion for wanting more out of life. Be a person that makes the most out of your time and every opportunity. Think things through and plan your daily activities. Always reevaluate your life and ask yourself "am I being productive in what I am currently doing?" Refocus your life and do those things that matter. What matters is different for different people. Different people have different motivations. Don't engage yourself into fights that waste your time and don't even matter. Some conflicts are between other people. Even family members, you can't fight their battles.

You need all your emotional energy for the situation that you will have to encounter. Become wise with your time and your emotional energy. Here you are getting all bent out of shape because your family member and his/her mate is fighting. Tell them to work out their own problems because nine times out of ten they will be back together.

It's easy to start off saying I will lose weight. It's easy to start that business. It's easy to start a lot of different things. The hard part is finishing what you started. Can you persevere when it's either food or this business? Can you persevere when you're working all day and don't feel like going to the gym or eating the right foods? To finish, it takes hard work and faith. Will you be determined in that marriage when he loses his job? Will you have the determination to finish college when you have to take care of kids or sick parents?

When things get hard and you are tempted to quit, you must shake it off each and every day. If you are putting in applications for different jobs and no one is calling back, you must think of creative ways to get in the door. Maybe you are going to have to go to the job, meet some people and shake some hands for the job you want. Maybe you will have to attend some networking events that lead you in the right direction. Are you determined even when there are setbacks to succeed? You can say you will start a business it will not be easy. You can say I do at the altar, the marriage will get rocky sometimes. To witness victory in any endeavor you undertake, it will take patience, determination, perseverance and a strong mentality. Along the road it will be each to get discouraged because of the challenges you will encounter. That's why faith and a bounce back attitude must be in your DNA. Just when you are about the cross the finish line to success, at that moment, when that breakthrough is at hand, here comes that setback you did not see coming. Here comes people lying on you and slandering your name. Here comes the health crisis. Here comes a lawsuit right out of the blue. If you keep fighting with a positive attitude and never give up, you can witness victory. Life is the best teach, so learn from past failures and mistakes. Grow into a good person and grow mentally and emotionally. Excel at the tasks you have been working each day to achieve. We all have different goals and things we are working on daily. Life will knock you down, and some knockdowns will have you wondering how you got into that situation. When you get knocked down, get back up and develop persistence and determination. Life will take the breath out of you, if you develop a determined spirit, you can raise above any setback. When things get hard, dig your heels in and with faith coupled with determination, fight for your goals.

Shake off the victim mentality and put on the armor of a victor. Develop a winning mentality through the thoughts you think. Develop an optimistic winning mentality in the thoughts you think. Don't sweat the small stuff. Don't sweat the tough. A week, month, year from now will not matter. It's a waste of time to live your life negative, filled with worry and discouraged. If you have lost your joy, do the things that you enjoy doing to reclaim your joy day to day. You may enjoy talking to certain people, go get your hair or toes done. Take a walk in the park. Read a good book. Take a vacation and see some stuff you have not seen before. Take steps to inject joy in your life. You can also take steps to rid yourself of toxic drama filled people. We are all good at different things. Find your creative spirit and use it to your advantage.

This book was written to bring hope for the lost, inspiration for the hunting and empowerment for the needy. Get in the habit of being a person that blesses and uplifts people. Limit the times of speaking badly about people. Go back to the days when we were little kids. If you don't have anything good to say, don't say anything at all. You have the power to become someone's miracle. You may say a work at the right time that will encourage someone. You have the power to restore the broken by the deeds that you do. It doesn't have to be big huge deeds. Something as simple as listening to someone's problems. Every day you can smile and be kind to a stranger. You can be an inspiration to a teenager who has lost his/her way along this path called life. When you plant good seed in people's life, the things you are hoping for will come to past. There are lots of ways you can help people. So many people are facing so many different kinds of hurt. We go to the gym to work out to make sure our bodies are in shape.

Where do you go to make sure that you are mentally in shape to deal with your problems day to day? You must recognize when you are overwhelmed with your problems and take the appropriate actions to get in better shape mentally, physically or emotionally. Some people you go around make you automatically feel down. Some people are full of drama and there is never any peace in their lives. People like this are usually our loved ones or someone close to us. You must develop skills to not let their negativity affect you in a bad way. You must develop skills to minimize arguments and tools to manage different situations and the moods people around you are feeling.

You look on the new every day and you see people who have not developed the correct coping strategies for dealing with problems they encounter. People that go commit suicide and kill everyone, if they had only stopped and talked to someone about their problems or looked at their situation with a different set of eyes, they would not have lost their minds. When you are living day-to-day, working, taking care of everything else, remember to take care of yourself first. You can be doing all these activities and before you know it, you can run out of emotional energy. It is good to meditate, listen to the word. It is good for you to exercise. It helps you stay connected with people and to interact with family and friends. Do activities that bring you joy. Recommend the book Surviving In Between to a person that needs encouragement or read your favorite book. Everyone has faced some suffering in his or her lives. We all go through different things. Developing the correct coping skill to deal with your problems is important. If you lose that job, if that relationship doesn't work, there will be some pain in your heart. Stop and think and analyze the situation. Most of the time it is not the end of the world.

The suffering is only temporary and things can get better if you keep the right attitude and thinking. Losing that job is not the end of the world. In fact, sometimes it can be a blessing in disguise. Maybe the job was stressing you out and now you have become less stressed. When one door closes another better one opens. By losing that job you can increase and get a better job with better pay and less stress. If that relationship did not work out that will just open the door up for you to meet someone better for you. The despair you are facing today is not permanent. When you are interacting with people on a daily basis look for ways to encourage them. When you listen to people when you encourage people you are showing compassion. When people come to you with the problem, make it a point not to judge. You may times feel helpless about a situation there is always help. We all face different kinds of stress that is a part of life. When you form good coping strategies to deal with your problems, you develop resilience to cope with adversity and deal with the challenges you encounter. When you face a challenge and successfully deal with the issues that are bothering you, your strength in confidence grows and you will be victorious in future challenges. Some situations will make you dig deep down inside of yourself. The challenges bring out good character and help us persevere while we are going through them.

Be a person that looks on the bright side when you are confronted with challenges. Challenges help you become wise in your dealing with life. You also develop wisdom. You need wisdom so you will not be foolish. When a soldier gets ready for war, the soldier has to prepare physically and mentally for all situations he/she may encounter. The soldier knows that going to war it will be ugly at times. The soldier knows there will be some surprises and challenges to encounter. The soldier realizes that pain is inevitable and that some tasks will be daunting and grueling. The soldier must be ready. In life you must prepare mentally and physically for the situations you will encounter. In life it will be ugly sometimes. You may lose your job or go through a divorce. Your loved one's may die. You may get sick. You may have legal problems. All kinds of different circumstances that can make life ugly. Just like the soldier in your life, there will be some tough challenges to face you must prepare your mind. Pain is inevitable suffering is optional.

When you prepare your mind, put it in your spirit to be a resilient overcomer. When you prepare for the worst, the worst never comes to pass. This is a book written to encourage you when the going gets tough. We need people to talk to because we have all had similar experiences in one-way or another. When we talk to someone, it eases the burden of the difficulties we are facing. Trouble can crush your spirit if you don't have a resilient mentality. If you develop a resilient mentality, then when trouble appears on your doorstep you develop a quiet confidence that at the end of the day everything will be right. If you had a tough childhood or grew up in a rough neighborhood, let that motivate to do well in life. Triumph over your bad circumstances and live a productive life. Different people have different ideas of what success is to them. You must believe in your mind that you are capable of overcoming becoming successful and happy. Where you are right now and where you trying to go plot your course of action with detail. When you plot your course of action, if you happen to get lost you can go back to goals and plot and get back on track. You may have ended up in jail for something you did not do and the circumstances have made you bitter towards the individual or individuals who lied on you, put it in your heart that you will not let unfair situations make you bitter or unforgiving. You can turn a bad situation into a blessing for yourself and others if you keep a positive mentality. While riding through a storm, it gets scary sometimes. It is lightning and you can hardly see. You see cars pulling over and you see some cars going faster. The thunder and lightning is bad, on top of that 18-wheelers are just speeding by with reckless abandonment. The best thing you can do during this storm is to do not panic. Keep your head clear during the storm. When you do not panic and you keep your head clear you make it through the storm. When it's thunder and lightning and you're driving, you have to focus on the road. You have to focus because if you start texting and getting distracted while you are driving in the storm, you could have a wreck.

What I'm saying is that when you are going

through the storm of life, you have to focus to make it through the storm. If you start getting distracted with doubt, fear and worry, you could crash. Whatever you focus on in life becomes bigger. Focus on faith, overcoming and improving your mental and physical state of mind

www.ingramcontent.com/pod-product-compliance
Lightning Source LLC
LaVergne TN
LVHW090116080426
835507LV00040B/918